TRANSPORT RESEARCH PROGRAM

DISTANCE AND DEVELOPMENT

Transport and Communications in India

WILFRED OWEN

TRANSPORT RESEARCH PROGRAM

DISTANCE AND DEVELOPMENT

Transport and Communications in India

THE BROOKINGS INSTITUTION
Washington, D.C.

Books published under the Transport Research Program

Wilfred Owen
Strategy for Mobility

Gary Fromm, Editor
Transport Investment and Economic Development

Edwin T. Haefele and Eleanor B. Steinberg
Government Controls on Transport: An African Case

George W. Wilson, Barbara R. Bergmann, Leon V. Hirsch, and Martin S. Klein
The Impact of Highway Investment on Development

Robert T. Brown
Transport and the Economic Integration of South America

Holland Hunter
Soviet Transport Experience: Its Lessons for Other Countries

Wilfred Owen
Distance and Development: Transport and Communications in India

© 1968 by
THE BROOKINGS INSTITUTION
1775 Massachusetts Avenue, N.W., Washington, D.C. 20036
Library of Congress Catalog Card Number 67–30599

Title page photograph: Margaret Bourke-White—*LIFE* Magazine

THE BROOKINGS INSTITUTION is an independent organization devoted to nonpartisan research, education, and publication in economics, government, foreign policy, and the social sciences generally. Its principal purposes are to aid in the development of sound public policies and to promote public understanding of issues of national importance.

The Institution was founded on December 8, 1927, to merge the activities of the Institute for Government Research, founded in 1916, the Institute of Economics, founded in 1922, and the Robert Brookings Graduate School of Economics and Government, founded in 1924.

The general administration of the Institution is the responsibility of a self-perpetuating Board of Trustees. The trustees are likewise charged with maintaining the independence of the staff and fostering the most favorable conditions for creative research and education. The immediate direction of the policies, program, and staff of the Institution is vested in the President, assisted by an advisory council chosen from the staff of the Institution.

In publishing a study, the Institution presents it as a competent treatment of a subject worthy of public consideration. The interpretations and conclusions in such publications are those of the author or authors and do not purport to represent the views of the other staff members, officers, or trustees of the Brookings Institution.

Foreword

Following his earlier general work, *Strategy for Mobility*, Wilfred Owen focuses attention in this volume specifically on the role of transport and communications in the economic and social problems of India. This is one of a series of books prepared during the five-year program of transport studies at Brookings made possible by a grant from the U.S. Agency for International Development.

The study of Indian transport was aided in the first instance by the invitation extended to the author by the World Bank to serve as a member of its economic mission to India in 1965–66. Special thanks are expressed to Bernard R. Bell, the mission director, and to Warren C. Baum, director of the Bank's transport division, for their help.

The author also wishes to acknowledge with gratitude the cheerful counsel of many Indian friends, who not only provided basic materials for the study but who joined in treks through many of the states of India where conditions could be studied first hand. While it is not possible to name all who helped, K. L. Luthra, Chief of Transport for the Planning Commission, deserves a special vote of thanks.

Finally, the author has relied on Inai Bradfield for excellent statistical research and general assistance and on Louise Axt and Joan Canzanelli for typing and editing. The index was prepared by Mrs. Rachel Johnson.

The reading committee for the study included Bernard E. Bell, International Bank for Reconstruction and Development, John P. Lewis, AID-India, and George W. Wilson, Indiana University. The book is a product of the Economic Studies Program, directed by Joseph A. Pechman. Views expressed do not presume to have the endorsement of the Agency for International Development or the World Bank and are not presented as the views of the trustees or staff members of the Brookings Institution or those who reviewed the manuscript.

KERMIT GORDON
President

November 1967
Washington, D.C.

Author's Preface

No country in the world confronts more urgent and staggering problems than India in its current struggle to survive. This country of half a billion people has passed through two decades of independence against almost insuperable odds. Among the barriers to progress were the basic poverty of the people, the overwhelming pressures of population on scarce resources, the great backlog of obsolescence in plant and equipment left by World War II, and the tremendous dislocations resulting from partition. Added to these handicaps in recent years have been the armed conflicts with China and Pakistan and the failure of the monsoon, which has parched the land and left hundreds of millions in the shadow of starvation.

The great wonder is not only that India lives but that in the short span of twenty years it has been able to show the most extraordinary physical achievements. Throughout the subcontinent are tens of thousands of newly constructed schools, hospitals, factories, power plants, irrigation works, agricultural developments, communication lines, office buildings, and housing developments. No one who has witnessed these changes could fail to be impressed with how much has been done.

But in the light of India's almost infinite needs, even this rate of accomplishment falls far short of minimum requirements, and the pressures for further achievement continue relentlessly. The struggle to determine whether the poorest one-sixth of the world can apply modern science and technology to save itself has just begun.

This study is concerned with one aspect of India's economic and social revolution—the means of transport and communications that make it possible to build a nation, to exploit its natural resources, to feed its people and its factories. The purpose is not to deprecate or to criticize policies and programs to date but to assess their impact on development and to inquire how more effective measures can be taken to provide the mobility on which much of the development program depends. The question is how best to proceed from here, using the fruits of technological innovation to make up for lost time.

The focus of this volume is on India, but studies of similar problems in other parts of the world make it clear that the conclusions have wider application. In every nation and in all stages of development, there is the same relation between economic progress and the capacity to move men, materials, and ideas. It is hoped that, by combining Western experience with the insights provided by sources within India and other less developed nations, the courses of action suggested in this book will be useful and relevant to many countries.

WILFRED OWEN

Contents

List of Tables

Appendix Tables

Explanatory Note on Special Terms

One *rupee* equals 13 cents (U.S.). Until the devaluation of June 1966, one rupee equaled 21 cents.

One *paisa* equals one-hundredth of one rupee.

One *crore* equals 10,000,000.

One *lakh* equals 100,000.

A *maund* is a varying measure of weight. In Uttar Pradesh one maund equals 82 pounds.

Octroi is a form of local tax and also the post where the tax is collected.

First Five-Year Plan   1951–56

Second Five-Year Plan   1956–61

Third Five-Year Plan   1961–66

Fourth Five-Year Plan   1966–71[*]

[*] Originally, the Fourth Five-Year Plan was intended to cover the period from April 1966 to March 1971. However, as this book goes to press the Government of India has postponed the plan period owing to the severe drought in 1965–66 and other problems.

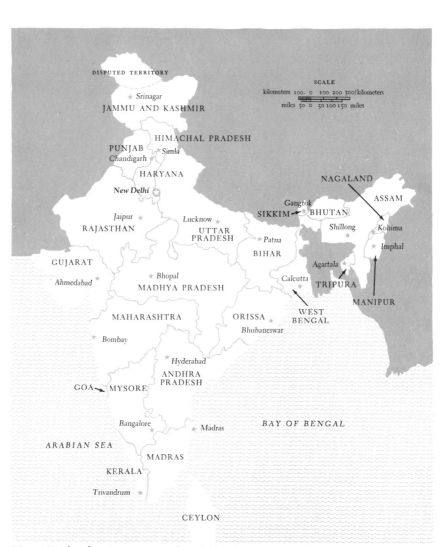

★ Srinagar
JAMMU AND KASHMIR

HIMACHAL PRADESH
PUNJAB
Chandigarh ★ Simla
HARYANA
New Delhi ⊛

SCALE
kilometers 100. 0 100 200 300|kilometers
miles 50 0 50 100 150 miles

NAGALAND
ASSAM
Gangtok
SIKKIM ★ BHUTAN
Shillong ★ Kohima
★ Imphal

Jaipur ★   Lucknow ★
RAJASTHAN   UTTAR
                PRADESH
                ★ Patna
                BIHAR

GUJARAT
Ahmedabad ★   ★ Bhopal
                MADHYA PRADESH
                                Agartala
                                ★ TRIPURA
                Calcutta ★
                                MANIPUR

MAHARASHTRA   ORISSA ★   WEST
                Bhubaneswar   BENGAL
★ Bombay

★ Hyderabad
ANDHRA
PRADESH
GOA ➤ MYSORE

Bangalore
★   ★ Madras   BAY OF BENGAL

ARABIAN SEA
MADRAS
KERALA
Trivandrum ★

CEYLON

Map of India showing states and capital cities.

CHAPTER I

The Task of Indian Transport

THE RECORD OF INDIA'S economic progress over the past decade and a half of planned development is a combination of impressive accomplishment and critical failure. Transportation has played a role in both.

Among the most visible signs of progress are the dams, power plants, steel mills, and factories, which could not have been built or put to use without the capacity to move large volumes of coal, iron ore, cement, stone, timber, and machinery.

Among the most obvious signs of failure are the poverty and isolation of the rural villages and the inability of India to feed itself. Without reliable farm-to-market transportation, among other things, it has not been possible to make the shift from subsistence farming to commercial agriculture.

Transportation is only one of the many ingredients necessary to accelerate the pace of economic progress, but in many instances it plays the key role, and in all cases it sets the limits. In India the limits can be seen quite clearly.

Transport Inadequacies

The first impression of India is that the principal occupation of the majority of Indians is moving themselves and their goods from one place to another. The streets of cities and towns and the roadways leading into them are a teeming mass of headloading pedestrians, beasts of burden, bullock carts, camel carts, and

Head-loading in an Indian village.

pushcarts. In the countryside, men and women and animals struggle to get things moved through mud and dust. It would be difficult to avoid the conclusion that the mobility of people and freight plays a vital role in nearly every aspect of India's daily life, and that lack of mobility places a heavy burden on industry, agriculture, and rural development.

India's low-capacity, high-cost transport is unequal to the tasks that modernization imposes on an ancient civilization. For the businessman, slow rail service and poor roads not only raise delivery costs and reduce the market area but add to these difficulties the burden of inventories large enough to compensate for unreliable deliveries. Transit is delayed when shipments move from one rail gauge to another, and service to intermediate points with inadequate pickup and delivery adds to the elapsed time. Congestion at the ports and the chaos of freight terminals in Bombay, Calcutta, Delhi, and other major urban centers cause major delays.

For many farmers, planting time may come and go before seed and fertilizer arrive, and it is often impossible to move produce fast enough to prevent spoilage, to move it where sales will yield adequate returns, or in some cases to move it at all. Rural villages without roads are also without medical services, veterinarians, or teachers. India's railways carry enormous volumes of bulk commodities, but the combination of high-density rail lines and low-capacity bullock carts has been unable to provide the total system needed to feed and supply one-sixth of the world's people.

Poor transport is also an obstacle to making effective use of India's natural resources. Much of the nation's wealth lies idle or is only partially utilized due to lack of access. Vast areas of arable land can be made more productive if fertilizers and other inputs for scientific agriculture can be delivered in significant amounts. One-fifth of the country is forest, containing a rich variety of hard and soft woods, but in many areas there is still no way to get these products moved. India is also rich in minerals, with one-fourth of the world's iron ore, large deposits of manganese and mica, and probably enough coal to last two centuries. But these possessions cannot be effectively exploited until the lack of transport or its high cost are overcome.

The extent of the transportation deficit in India is indicated by comparisons with transport resources in the rest of the world. India accounts for 16 percent of the world's people but for only 4 percent of its improved roads, 2 percent of its rail freight, and 1 percent of its trucks and buses. Even on the national road net, eight out of ten miles of highways have only one lane. Among the more than half a million Indian villages, only one out of nine is served by an all-weather road. There are fewer trucks in India than there are in Los Angeles.

Everywhere the evidence suggests an imbalance in the transport program. Attention has been focused primarily on intercity rail movements, but the transport problems of agriculture, rural development, consumer goods industries, retail trade, and the cities have been neglected. This imbalance goes a long way toward explaining the inadequate level of food production, the inaccessibility of most of India's farms, and the lost opportunities for economic development that have been the result of failure to overcome the barriers imposed by distance.

The tasks of raising living standards in a nation where average per capita income for half a billion people is little over $1.00 per week impose a staggering burden on the Indian economy and the transport system that serves it. The outlook has been particularly disturbing since Third Plan growth turned out to be less than half the target rate, and the last year of the Plan ended with a 4 percent decline in national income. These difficulties were precipitated by the worst drought in one hundred years, which canceled many of the gains that had been won in the battle to feed the nation. A million tons of food grains had to be imported per month to avert starvation. Failure of the monsoon was the major problem, but its impact was magnified by the underlying weakness of the economy, including the absence of communications in the broad sense of moving men, materials, and ideas.

Transport Accomplishments

But the picture is by no means completely dismal, for in many important respects transport has successfully provided essential support for the progress of the Indian economy. The transport system has helped to meet industrial production targets which together added 146 percent to the output of Indian industry between 1950 and 1965. Very rapid growth took place in the output of steel, aluminum, chemicals, and petroleum. Installed electric power capacity quadrupled during this period, and 50,000 towns and villages were supplied with electricity. More than a quarter of a million schools were constructed to accommodate 44 million additional children, and 45,000 new health centers helped to raise the average life expectancy from 32 to 50 years. (See Table I–1.) These accomplishments required material movements on a large scale, and were particularly dependent on the Indian railways.

TABLE I–1.   *Growth of the Indian Economy, 1950–66*

Selected items	1950–51	1965–66	Index 1965–66 (1950/51 = 100)
National income (billions of U.S. dollars)	18.8[a]	31.8[a,b]	169[b]
Per capita income (1948–49 rupees)	247.5	314.4[b]	127[b]
Population (millions)	356	492	138
Food grains (million tons)	54.9	72.3	132
Coal (million tons)	32.8	70.0	213
Iron ore (million tons)	3.0	23.0	767
Finished steel (million tons)	1.0	4.6	460
Nitrogeneous fertilizers (thousand tons)	9	233	2,589
Schools (thousands)	231	505	219
Students (thousands)	23,500	67,700	288
Primary health centers	2,800[c]	48,000	1,714

Sources: Government of India, Planning Commission, *Fourth Five Year Plan: A Draft Outline* (1966), pp. 8–11, 13, 28; national income data from Government of India, *Economic Survey 1965–66* (1966), Table 1–1.

a. 1948–49 rupee equivalent.
b. Preliminary estimates of 1964–65.
c. 1960–61.

Agricultural output has also shown important long-run gains, and transport has been a factor in making this possible. Although India currently faces a food crisis, food grain production from 1950 to 1965 increased 30 percent, and the peak harvest of 1964–65 was 62 percent above 1950.[1] During this time the area under major cultivation has been expanded by nearly 14 million acres, and fertilizer consumption is ten times what it was fifteen years ago. These accomplishments indicate what Indian agriculture might be expected to achieve with a return to more normal weather and with a system of rural transport capable of supporting intensive cultivation on a large scale.

As a result of these gains, the country's net national product rose 70 percent in 15 years, accompanied by a 170 percent increase in freight transport that helped to make this possible. Freight moving by rail more than doubled in a decade, and truck transport quadrupled. Every day the Indian railways operate 10,000 trains, load half a million tons of freight, and carry five million passengers. Jet airliners now serve the major cities, and air traffic is four times what it was five years ago. Trucks are cutting medium and short-haul transport time to a fraction of what it takes by rail, and pipelines moving both crude oil and petroleum products are the latest additions to the transport network.

To arrive at this level of achievement has required a very large commitment of resources to transport. Transport accounted for approximately one-fifth of all public and private investments in the first three plan periods. One-fourth of all public funds spent for development were allocated for this purpose. (See Table I–2.)

Future Transport Burdens

Indian transport has somehow made possible the substantial gains in production to date, but the increasing tasks already in

---

[1] Food grain production for 1964–65 was 89 million tons.

TABLE I–2. *Allocations of Public Funds for Transport in Indian Development Plans*

Purpose	Expenditures (in percent)		
	First Plan	Second Plan	Third Plan
Railways	55	68	67
Roads and road transport	30	21	24
Inland water transport	. . .[a]	. . .[a]	. . .[a]
Ports and harbors	6	3	5
Shipping	4	5	2
Civil air transport	6	4	3
Total[b]	100	100	100
Transport as percent of total public expenditures	24.3	25.8	23.1

Source: Appendix Table 1. For data on public and private investment in transport in relation to total investment, see Appendix Table 2.

a. Less than 1 percent.

b. Exceeds 100 because of rounding.

sight pose new and critical problems for the future. The population—500 million in 1966—can be expected to reach 625 million by 1975. Each month, an additional million people will have to be fed and supplied. The over-all goal for the Fourth Plan is a 48 percent increase in national income over the 1965–66 figure. Food grain production is to be increased by one-third, industrial production by two-thirds, and the number of jobs by 19 million. (See Appendix Table 4.)

Coal consumption is expected to double between 1960 and 1970. Large increases in other bulk commodities, including iron ore, chemicals, and building materials, will have to be transported. The volume of these heavy bulk commodities will increase as new industries begin operations and as plants now operating below capacity because of material shortages are, it is hoped, able to increase production.

Transport demand will also be augmented by large increases in fertilizer production, and by the distribution to farmers of both domestic and imported supplies. The objective of raising rural living standards will stimulate the production of a large variety of consumer goods, and this new emphasis will add to the need for fast transit and efficient handling.

Targets for the Fourth Plan indicate the nature of the transportation problems to be coped with. Principal tasks will be to promote exports and replace imports; to increase the income of the rural population; to support the production of such farm goods as insecticides, agricultural implements, pumps, diesel engines, and tractors to help maximize agricultural output; and to expand the supplies of essential mass consumption goods, including textiles, sugar, drugs, and kerosene.[2]

Altogether, these targets imply not only a more rapid growth in transport demand than the average increases of previous plan periods, but a shift in the location and type of transport to be provided. Based on past experience, the stepped-up rate of growth will mean an even more rapid increase in the freight burden. The Planning Commission conservatively estimates that freight traffic in 1970 will be 85 percent above the 1965 level, an increase of 200 million tons.

The level of economic activity projected for the Fourth Plan will mean a 50 percent increase in railway freight traffic during the period, and railway passenger travel is expected to be up one-quarter. Estimates of increased freight traffic by motor truck are higher than for rail, with a rise of 82 percent over the five years. Two-thirds more tonnage will be moving through the major ports. (See Table I–3.)

Some Recent Policy Conclusions

These figures indicate the nature and magnitude of Fourth Plan transport needs. How they are to be met depends partly on the programming of development funds and partly on policies governing the role of transport as an instrument for economic development. India's transport policies have recently been sub-

[2] Government of India, Planning Commission, *Fourth Five Year Plan: A Draft Outline* (1966), p. 17. These targets are subject to further revision.

TABLE I–3.   *Fourth Plan Transport Projections*

Sector	Fourth Plan	Percentage increase over Third Plan achievements
Railway freight traffic (million tons)	308	50
Railway ton-kilometers (billions)	162[a]	42
Railway passenger-kilometers (billions)	126[a]	27
Road ton-kilometers (billions)	60	82
Road passenger-kilometers (billions)	120	50
Surfaced roads (thousand kilometers)	334	18
Number of buses (thousands)	100	43
Number of trucks (thousands)	425	70
Traffic in major ports (million tons)	83	66
Shipping tonnage (million GRT)	3[b]	95
Civil air transport (million revenue ton-kilometers):		
Air India	290	87
Indian Airlines	213	97

Source: Government of India, Planning Commission, *Fourth Five Year Plan: A Draft Outline* (1966), pp. 304, 310.
a. Data supplied by the Planning Commission.
b. Available capacity.

jected to the scrutiny of a government Committee on Transport Policy and Coordination. This Committee, which began its work in 1959, was established to determine "what broadly should be the long-term transport policy of the country" and how transport needs could be met "in an efficient and economic manner consistent with the larger interests of the country."[3] The Committee initiated a number of studies of transport within the country and abroad, and its final report took a forward-looking stand on many of the basic issues raised during the past decade by India's approach to transport development. It is the first official statement to recognize the inherent limitations of the

[3] Government of India, Planning Commission, *Committee on Transport Policy and Coordination: Final Report* (1966), p. 2. The Committee included key officials from the Ministries of Industry, Finance, Economic Affairs, Railways, Transport, and the Planning Commission, and from the Administrative Staff College, Hyderabad.

railways, the importance of road transport as a major segment of the transport system, and the necessity for a more vigorous attack on transport problems that inhibit agriculture and rural development.

A vast increase in road services is called for, the Committee concluded, in order to integrate the rural sector of the economy with the urban and industrial sector. Among past policies and practices rejected by the Committee are restrictive truck licensing, placing distance limits on truck operations, failing to provide adequate resources for roadbuilding, and imposition of vexatious taxes such as the local duties, or octroi, and passenger and goods levies. The report calls for programming road expenditures on the basis of industry and other development needs, and special emphasis is placed on the importance of roads in areas where intensive agricultural development plans are being undertaken or where new resources such as irrigation and power have come into use.

Other policy conclusions recommend improving the terms of motor vehicle financing, establishing state highway departments, allocating more state revenues to village roads, and seeking solutions to the transport and land-use planning problems of large cities. The Committee also recognized that controls on transport should be viewed as positive means to exploit the promise of new technology and not, as in the past, to protect the railways. Accordingly, the report recommends the licensing of interstate trucking by the central government, to eliminate the bargaining among states for local advantages.

At the same time, however, the Committee proposed that the states control minimum and maximum rates for trucking services. This measure would be a serious blow to road transport's potential capabilities for promoting a more dynamic economy. For freedom to adjust to varying conditions of supply and demand is a key to the effective operation and expansion of this flexible new transport medium.

Notwithstanding the proposal for extending regulation, road transport was generally accorded far more favorable treatment in the Committee's report than in any previous deliberations on the subject. This changing attitude was apparent in the conclusion that railways are inherently best suited to long-distance movements and the carriage of bulk commodities, and that further extension of rail lines must now be limited to the special needs of these types of traffic. The report also recognizes that railway branch lines will have to be studied for possible abandonment and the substitution of road services. The need for new technology is emphasized, along with further adjustment of railway rates to yield a return comparable to capital earnings in other sectors. The railways are called upon to pay greater attention to consumer needs through efforts to market railway services, and commutation is viewed as an integral part of metropolitan transport systems.

Fourth Plan for Transport

To bring these policy changes into being and to accommodate the increased burdens that transport must bear in the next five years are the tasks that will have to be carried out through the operations of the Fourth Plan, which substantially increases the availability of public funds for transport and introduces important changes in emphasis. Transport money is 37 percent above Third Plan outlays, and is equivalent to $3.6 billion for the five years on the basis of the recently devalued rupee. Altogether the transport budget comprises 17 percent of total public sector outlays. Of this, the railways will receive half for the purchase of locomotives and other equipment and for double tracking, centralized traffic control, automatic signaling, and construction of new lines. The highway program, totaling somewhat over one-fourth of the transport outlay, is aimed at correcting some of the worst deficiencies in the national highways. Half the highway allocation will go to this national system, much of it to build major bridges and convert one-lane facilities to two lanes. The remainder will be spent for roads under state jurisdiction, and will add about 50,000 kilometers to the system.

Other targets include half a million trucks and buses to be in operation by the end of the Fourth Plan, a two-thirds increase over Third Plan levels. There is also provision for replacing obsolete shipping tonnage and for adding substantially to present capacity in the hope that half of all overseas trade may be moving in Indian ships ten years from now.

The Fourth Plan introduces important changes in emphasis. The rail share is 52 percent of available resources, compared with 67 percent in the Third Plan, while roads and road transport increase their share of the total from 24 to 30 percent. In absolute amounts there is a 71 percent increase in highway outlays and a 150 percent increase in the aviation budget, compared to only a 7 percent increase in railway expenditures. (See Table I–4.)

The transport program, then, seems to be moving in the right direction to correct some of the past imbalances. But a closer

TABLE I–4.   *Fourth Plan Outlays of Public Funds for Transportation*

Sector	Outlays (in crores of rupees)[a]	Percentage distribution	Percentage increase over Third Plan outlays
Railways[b]	1,410	52	7
Roads	760	28	71
Road transport	65	2	141
Ports[c]	242	9	155
Shipping	90	3	120
Inland water transport	13	1	333
Civil air transport[d]	125	5	150
Tourism	25	1	317
Total transport	2,730	100[e]	37
Total development expenditures	16,000		85

Source: Government of India, Planning Commission, *Fourth Five Year Plan: A Draft Outline* (1966), pp. 43, 297.
  a. One crore = 10,000,000. The official rate of exchange was 4.7 rupees to one U.S. dollar until 1966, when the rupee was devalued to 7.5 per dollar.
  b. In addition, 684 crores of rupees are expected to be made available from the Railway Depreciation Reserve Fund.
  d. Includes 40 crores of rupees from depreciation funds of the air corporations and also
  c. Includes expenditures on lighthouses and on Farakka Barrage Project in the Fourth Plan. expenditures on meteorology.
  e. Because of rounding, total exceeds 100.

look reveals that in important respects the program does not take into account some of the critical goals established for the development plan, and does not appear designed to bring about the changes recommended by the Committee on Transport Policy and Coordination. Many of the elements necessary to support Plan objectives are included, but the program as a whole lacks the necessary linking with specific targets and reforms.

Almost entirely overlooked are the transport measures that could help support efforts to achieve India's Fourth Plan goals for agriculture and rural development. There are no specific provisions for the delivery of agricultural inputs or for marketing agriculture produce, and failure of the central government to share in responsibility for these aspects of the agricultural effort may well mean that targets for fertilizer distribution and increased food marketing will not be attained.

The Fourth Plan program is also silent on road-rail coordination, one of the Committee's principal objectives. It does not exploit the possibilities of integrated freight services by road and rail, nor does it focus on promoting the specialized services which the Committee has concluded the railways are best suited to perform. The Plan is essentially a listing of what is to be accomplished by each method of transport and by each administrative agency, without attempting to determine the best *total* system that technological innovations make possible. These weaknesses leave the impression that some urgently needed changes in Indian transport are not likely to materialize in the period of the Fourth Plan.

India's principal transport tasks have three main aspects. The first involves the main intercity routes that serve industry primarily. Here, the need is to modernize and operate major intercity transport facilities as an integral supporting system for industrialization. Second is the local rural transport net that supports agriculture. Here, at the local rural level, transport will have to be made part of a total strategy for increasing the food supply and for bridging the gap between the urban industrial sector and the rural areas, in which four-fifths of the population lives. Third is the transport systems needed for viable cities. In urban areas transport can help lay out new patterns of urban settlement that will ameliorate the congestion of the metropolis and provide new market towns for commercial agriculture.

No country has been able to resolve to universal satisfaction the many complex issues that arise in the formulation of transport policy. One reason is that technological changes in transport affect large and durable investments that involve powerful interests. It is not surprising, therefore, that the preoccupation of Indian transport policy is with tensions inside the transport field rather than with transport's capabilities for promoting external development. This introversion, which is at the very heart of India's transport problems, has diverted attention from the realization that transport can provide a potent tool for economic growth and for the improvement of living conditions. How transport changes will affect transport tends to become the focus of concern, rather than how these changes can help feed the hungry, transform rural society, provide new jobs, create business opportunities, reduce production costs, stimulate exports, and achieve a viable pattern of urbanization.

The Committee on Transport Policy and Coordination opened the way for a fresh approach. It is now clear that "the significance of the transport sector lies not only in the specific services it renders, but even more in the unifying and integrating influence it exerts upon the economy, enhancing productivity [and] introducing new stimuli to economic activity. . . ."[1]

The period of transport rehabilitation following independence has come to a close, and the opportunity to view the transport function more broadly in relation to economic and social goals has arrived. The purpose of this study is to analyze the directions in which Indian transport policy should move to release dynamic new forces for India's economic lift-off, and to suggest in broader perspective how distance affects development.

[1] Government of India, Planning Commission, *Committee on Transport Policy and Coordination: Final Report*, p. 6.

CHAPTER II

Intercity Transport and the Development Program

THE GREAT DISTANCES separating India's major cities and the location of her natural resources have necessitated long supply lines to meet the needs of an increasingly urban-industrial society. India is only 40 percent as large as the United States, but its major centers of population are far apart. It is over a thousand miles from Bombay to Calcutta and close to a thousand from Bombay to Delhi. From Madras to Delhi is 1,500 miles. Food grains travel hundreds of miles to feed the urban population. Coal, the largest single item of traffic on the railways, moves all the way across the country from the Bengal-Bihar district to Bombay, where one-third of India's manufacturing capacity is concentrated.

Altogether, the main arteries of Indian commerce are carrying a quarter of a billion tons of freight per year to connect the major cities, to feed them, and to supply their industrial plants with fuel and raw materials. The railways have provided most of this support, assisted by inland water traffic in some areas and by limited coastal movements of coal, cement, and general cargo. Road transport has played a strong complementary role in recent years, particularly in the movement of machinery, consumer goods, and farm traffic. Road and rail transport also share almost equally in the movement of passengers, with long-distance air services playing an important supplementary role. (See Appendix Table 5 for the Indian transport system's basic facilities and equipment.)

15

Freight Traffic Patterns

While India's national income rose 58 percent from 1950 to 1964, the rise in road and rail freight traffic was 170 percent. (See Table II–I.) Approximately 30 percent more freight had to

TABLE II–1. *Freight Traffic and Economic Trends, 1950–64*
(Index, 1950–51 = 100)

Year	Road and rail[a]	National income[b]	Industrial production	Population
1950–51	100.0	100.0	100.0	100.0
1955–56	138.1	118.4	125.0	109.2
1960–61	211.8	144.1	177.0	121.1
1961–62	226.2	147.6	189.4	123.6
1962–63	253.3	151.1	203.7	126.9
1963–64	269.7	157.5	222.6	129.9

Source: Government of India, Planning Commission, *Committee on Transport Policy and Coordination: Final Report* (1966), p. 13.
a. Based on ton-miles.
b. In 1948–49 prices.

be moved for every 10 percent added to total income. The railways, which are the largest public enterprise in the country, carried three-fourths of this intercity traffic. They operate 35,000 miles of routes with three different gauges, but the broad gauge lines are by far the most important, comprising half the mileage and moving 80 percent of the freight.[1] Seventy percent of rail freight tonnage is accounted for by seven types of shipments: coal, iron and steel, cement, limestone, metallic ores, food grains, and petroleum.

During the first three five-year plans, freight movement on the highways increased five-fold while rail traffic increased two and

[1] The meter gauge lines make up 44 percent of the system and the narrow gauges 7 percent. Traffic on the system is heavily concentrated: 18 percent of the network carries 61 percent of the load. Sections on this heavily traveled part of the system average 10,000 tons of traffic per day.

a half times. As a result, although truck transport was only about 12 percent of the combined road-rail total at the beginning of the period, it was 23 percent fifteen years later. (See Table II–2.)

TABLE II–2.   *Freight Traffic by Rail and Road, 1950–66*

Year	Freight volume		
	Rail	Road	Total
	Billion ton-kilometers		
1950–51	44	6	50
1955–56	60	9	69
1960–61	88	17	105
1965–66	114	35	149
	Percentage		
1950–51	88	12	100
1955–56	87	13	100
1960–61	84	16	100
1965–66	77	23	100
	Index		
1950–51	100	100	100
1955–56	135	163	138
1960–61	199	316	212
1965–66	258	636	300

Sources: Government of India, Planning Commission, *Committee on Transport Policy and Coordination: Final Report* (1966), p. 10; data for 1965–66 supplied by Planning Commission.

The shift from rail to road has been primarily in high-value commodities and perishables. In all parts of the country, trucks are hauling rice, fruits and vegetables, textiles, machinery, iron and steel, cement, building materials, canned goods, and processed food. On the route from Delhi to Bombay, approximately 40 percent of total tonnage represents products of agriculture, and the largest single class of freight is fruits and vegetables moving over relatively short distances. (See Appendix Table 6.) At the same time, the railways have become increasingly involved in the movement of bulk products. They account for 89 percent of all the coal that moves, 71 percent of the iron ore,

73 percent of the cement, and 62 percent of all petroleum products.[2]

The loss of some high-rated traffic to the truck has hurt the railways, and the prospect of further diversions poses a continuing financial threat. Over half of rail freight revenues are still derived from manufactures and other high-rated traffic, and the questions are how far the shift from rail to road can be expected to go, how these trends will affect the railways, and what they will mean for rail and road investment plans.

With the development of new methods of mechanical transport, the pattern of goods movement has changed in all countries of the world. The degrees of change have differed, but the directions have been much the same. Typically the railways are making moderate to substantial gains in volume, but the percentage of rail freight in the total is declining. Truck transport, on the other hand, is registering very sharp gains both in absolute figures and in its proportion of total freight. Air transport and pipelines are filling new needs, while water transport appears to be experiencing moderate growth.

Thus, in Japan between 1956 and 1965, the total increase in ton-kilometers of freight moved was 93 percent. Rail traffic increased 21 percent, and truck transport 346 percent. (See Appendix Table 7.) In the Soviet Union, ton-kilometers by railway tripled in volume between 1950 and 1965, as did river transport, but truck transport increased seven-fold and pipeline transport thirty-fold. In 1940 the railways of the U.S.S.R. accounted for 85 percent of total freight, the highways for less than 2 percent, and pipelines for less than 1 percent. By 1965, the rail share had fallen to 80 percent, with pipelines and trucking each up to 6 percent.[3]

Transport trends in the United States also reveal a faster expansion of road transport relative to rail. While all forms of

[2] Government of India, Planning Commission, *Committee on Transport Policy and Coordination: Final Report* (1966), p. 11.

[3] See Holland Hunter, "The Soviet Transport Sector," in *New Directions in the Soviet Economy*, Studies Prepared for the Subcommittee on Foreign Economic Policy of the Joint Economic Committee, 89 Cong. 2 sess. (1966), p. 576.

Moving freight by air.
Air-India

transport have shown substantial increases since 1950, the railway share of total freight has fallen from 56 to 43 percent, with trucks increasing their share from 16 to 23 percent and pipelines moving up from 12 to 19 percent. (For trends in United States and Soviet transport, see Appendix Tables 8 and 9.) These trends are paralleled by what is taking place in passenger movement: in addition to the growth of private automobile ownership, the trend in transport by public carrier generally favors road over rail and, in recent years, air over surface.

Modernizing the Railways

For India the experience of other countries is a reminder that with today's wider choice of transport technology, each method will tend to concentrate on those services for which it has a clear competitive advantage. The corollary is that every effort should be made to phase out as quickly as possible those services which cannot in the long run hope to provide an acceptable level of economy or quality.

In other words, India should avoid the use of resources to provide services by rail if these can be performed more satisfactorily by road, or vice versa. It is equally important to prevent traffic from shifting from one mode to another if the shift is due not to inherent capabilities but to temporary conditions that need to be remedied.

Clearly a comparative advantage for the railways lies in the transportation of large volumes of heavy traffic at low cost, and they need to concentrate on doing this priority job effectively. Railways could handle many other types of traffic efficiently in conjunction with other modes, especially trucks, but would have little hope of success if they tried to do the whole job alone.

Steps are being taken to improve the inherent capabilities of India's railway transport and to strengthen its competitive position. Diesel locomotives are replacing steam, larger bogie freight cars are taking the place of the small four-wheelers, automatic track signal control is being extended, and some meter gauge lines are being converted to broad gauge. It is estimated that 5,000 kilometers of line will be electrified by 1970, and 10,000 by 1975. By 1970, freight hauled by steam engines will have declined to half the total, the rest being hauled by electric and diesel locomotives.[4]

How much these steps will actually strengthen the position of the railways depends on whether they improve services holding real promise for the future. One promising possibility is the use of unit trains for moving large quantities of bulk commodities between points of major traffic origin and destination, such as mines, ports, and large industrial users. Unit trains perform like a giant conveyer belt, bypassing intermediate freight yards and moving very large volumes of bulk traffic at high speed.[5] They greatly reduce the cost of moving coal, iron ore, and food grains, and yield substantial dividends for both the railways and their customers. India has introduced some unit trains, but there has been no effort to initiate extensive operations of this type.

Another goal which new investments might seek is to reduce the time required for transit on the Indian railways. A full carload may take six weeks to get from Madras to Delhi—an over-all speed of 1.5 miles per hour. A small shipment between terminals off the main line may take six months. Not only excessive delay but the uncertainty of when delivery will be made or when the journey will start make it difficult to conduct business economically. Much of the time loss is due to the absence of coordination between railways and trucks. Freight may move at reasonable speed on the main lines, but the time spent in terminals and yards may sharply reduce total transit

[4] A discussion of improved operation of Indian and Soviet railways is contained in Holland Hunter, *Soviet Transport Experience: Its Lessons for Other Countries* (Brookings Institution, 1968).

[5] On one rail line in the United States, 150 round trips per year were accomplished on a unit train route compared to 18 round trips accomplished with conventional trains. Volumes are as high as 12,000 tons per train.

speed. The solution lies in a variety of related measures, including terminal modernization, better communications, and use of trucks for pickup and delivery.

The development of container traffic is a major potential for overcoming some of the inherent inadequacies of the railways and for avoiding unnecessary investments in highways, trucks, and railway cars. Containers can reduce handling costs, paper work, time delays in pickup and delivery, and losses from breakage and pilferage. Investment in flatcars for container traffic permits the line-haul economy of the railways to be realized along with fast transfer and the door-to-door service of the truck. Containers could be interchanged among all methods of transport and between rail gauges to provide an important degree of coordination in Indian transport.

A variation of container movement is piggyback operations—carrying truck trailers on railway flatcars. Piggyback service in the United States has been found to be less costly than truck movement for all hauls over 100 miles. The cost of transporting 20 tons of goods 500 miles by trailer-on-flatcar was found to be only half as much as by over-the-road truck, and 30 percent less than by conventional boxcar.[6] Savings through containerization are generally comparable to those by piggyback. Charges for moving 10 tons of glassware approximately 500 miles in the United States by container are less than half the rate by boxcar.[7]

Another possibility for time-and-cost saving lies in railway communications, which greatly need improvement if they are to contribute to efficient utilization of equipment and reasonable standards of service. Indian railway management is fed information on traffic demands and available capacity by telephone facilities, which are much too slow to provide current information. Modern microwave communications plus the computerization of information on traffic demands and rolling stock availability could greatly increase rail performance. In the United

[6] E. C. Poole, in *Railway Age*, August 26, 1957, pp. 16–20.
[7] *Traffic Management*, Vol. 17, No. 2 (February 1965).

States, computerized traffic control has made it possible to get 40 percent more use per freight car.

Integrating Rail and Road

Further promise for speeding service lies in the effective use of motor trucking to supplement or supplant railway operations. The railways could make contractual arrangements with trucking firms for pickup and delivery service, or they could operate the service themselves. Trucks could also be used off the main line, where traffic is light and where a multiplicity of pickup points and destinations creates long delays on the railways. Some moves have been made by the Indian railways to operate their own trucks, but the effort has not been popular either with railway officials or the states. Railway administrators have not been easily won over to the idea that they are in the transportation business, and the states have not encouraged railways to engage in truck transport, since the rail system is a function of the central government while road transport is under state control.

In any event, effective rail transport requires a shift of small shipments and short hauls from rail to road, and only truck transport can furnish these services with the necessary speed and frequency. Trucks are also favored for fragile goods, since protective packaging may make rail costs excessive. While these alternative road services could continue to be provided exclusively by private truckers, the pressures are mounting for operation of some road freight services in the public sector. The railways have the managerial skills and the facilities to bring this about, and the integration of public sector freight services in this way seems preferable to the proposed interstate trucking lines that would operate under a separate public corporation. Furthermore, the need is not primarily for interstate trucking but for local pickup and delivery and for branch line services. If these services could be furnished by an integrated rail-highway

Moving hay by cart.

Public carrier truck at railway siding.

operation, the railways would benefit from road transport development rather than be put at a disadvantage.

The transport company as a means of integrating road and rail and other transport services is being developed in varying degree in other countries. The Canadian National Railways in the public sector and the Canadian Pacific Railways in the private sector operate not only rail services but trucks, ships, and aircraft. Rate policies are designed to encourage the economic use of each method. In Japan, Nippon Express, originally established by the Japanese National Railways to provide truck pickup and delivery service to and from rail stations, operates trucking services throughout the country. Some method of providing an integrated road-rail service in India seems essential to the financial future of the railways, the provision of satisfactory service, and the avoidance of excessive transport investment.

Road Transport: Growth and Inadequacies

The vitality of the railways depends on selective modernization where new techniques prove economically desirable, combined with the integration of rail operations with other transport media. It is especially true that a strong railway system depends on good road transport. Trucks can take over the short hauls, small shipments, perishables, fragile goods, and other traffic that moves by railways at a loss. The road transport revolution needs to be accelerated to permit an economic sorting out of traffic that can be advantageous to both carriers.

Since the beginning of the First Plan period, India has increased its surfaced roads by 82 percent; in the past ten years, 10,000 kilometers of newly surfaced roads have been constructed annually. The number of motor vehicles in the country had risen to over a million units by 1966, and commercial vehicles on the highways had nearly tripled during the preceding decade and a half. (See Table II–3.)

TABLE II-3. *Growth of Road Network and Motor Vehicles, 1951–66*
(In thousands)

Year	Kilometers of roads		
	Surfaced	Unsurfaced	Total
1951	156	242	398
1956	182	314	495
1961	234	471	705
1962	246	499	745
1963	251	501	752
1966 (est.)	284	674	958
Percentage increase, 1951–66	82	179	141

Year	Trucks and buses in operation		
	Trucks	Buses	Total
1950–51	82	34	116
1955–56	119	47	166
1960–61	168	57	225
1965–66	255	73	328
Percentage increase, 1950–66	211	115	183

Sources: Data on length of roads from Government of India, Planning Commission, *Committee on Transport Policy and Coordination: Final Report* (1966), p. 62; and on numbers of trucks and buses from the Planning Commission.

The growth of road transport in India, however, has not always been a welcome trend among government officials, and the progress of road transport in India has been less rapid than in other major nations of the world. (See Appendix Table 10.) This relatively new technology is seen as wasteful of resources and as in costly competition with the rail transportation system to which India is heavily committed.

Viewed in the larger context of Indian economic development, however, the expansion of motor transport will not be detrimental to the railways because it will play an essential role in the expansion of agricultural development and industry. The limited accomplishments to date have had impressive results. Roads have opened up new geographic areas and new areas of economic opportunity. Motorized transport has begun to supplement the bullock cart and to provide an extensive network of passenger travel, thus beginning the task of building the necessary economic and social ties between rural India and the urban-industrial economy. In manufacturing, too, shippers have found that it is often cheaper to pay more for road transport in order to pay less in total distribution costs.

There can be no revolution in agriculture without a revolution in road transport. The expansion of consumer goods production will also require trucking services, and on a large network of lightly traveled routes the motor vehicle rather than the railway will be the only practical method of transport. The resulting growth of highway transport will have far-reaching economic effects, including the creation of jobs and new business opportunities. All of this will add to the total volume of traffic in which the railways share. The railways will continue to carry large absolute amounts, but a proportionately smaller part of the total.

Obstacles to the efficiency and economic expansion of motor trucking thus also impede the growth of the Indian economy and of railway traffic resulting from economic growth. One of these impediments is the state of the highways. Four out of five miles of national highways are one-lane. There is not yet a completely connected national system; 400 kilometers of gaps are yet to be closed, and more than 50 major bridges need to be built. Culverts and bridges are often weak, and pavements inadequate. State and district roads, which comprise the rest of the main road system, are even poorer than the national highways. Narrow and bumpy, often flooded during the monsoon, they are severely limited in load-carrying capacity and permissible speed. And on the vastly larger network of village access roads, conditions are generally so poor that motorized traffic is impossible.

Another major handicap to efficient road transport is the inadequacy, in both quantity and quality, of available commercial vehicles. The ratio of trucks to population is considerably below that in other poor countries. Much of the fleet is always immobilized by the breakdown of over-aged vehicles, lack of parts, and inadequate repair facilities. Many over-the-road vehicles are too small to furnish economical transport, and there are not enough small pickup trucks to meet the special needs of agriculture.

Truck and bus production is now only 40,000 units a year, little more than enough to maintain the present operating fleet. Assuming that ten percent of the vehicles now operating will have to be retired each year, replacement needs will be approximately 33,000 annually. Estimates of a sharp rise in goods movement and bus travel over the next five years (80 percent for trucking and 50 percent for bus travel) indicate that new vehicle requirements will total 242,000 during the Fourth Plan,[8] without taking local farm transport needs into account. Annual output will have to be increased to well above 100,000 units by 1970, two and a half times the 1965 level.

Truck tractor and semi-trailer combinations could furnish India with substantially lower-cost transport, but such vehicles cannot now be operated due to the low capacity of bridges on most of the system. The loss to the economy resulting from this constraint is considerable. The estimated cost of hauling light merchandise in conventional 8-ton single unit trucks is substantially greater by road than by rail for any trip over 100 kilometers. At 250 kilometers, trucking with this equipment costs twice as much as by rail. But when a 13-ton tractor semi-trailer is used, transport cost is about the same by road as by rail up to 250 kilometers, and the speed and service by truck are likely to be far superior. (See Table II–4.) The significance of these comparisons is not in their effect on the competitive position of road and rail but in the fact that, with larger vehicles available, shippers now depending on small trucks could cut their costs in half.

India's tax and regulatory policies also reduce the efficiency of road transport. Licenses for interstate trucking operations are made available only on a reciprocal basis, with each state limiting the permits it issues to the number another will grant. The number of licenses issued is thus the result of laborious bar-

[8] Memorandum from the Planning Commission, Government of India, April 1966.

TABLE II–4. *Comparative Costs of Road and Rail Haulage*
(In rupees per ton)

Distance in kilometers	Railways[a]		Road[b]	
	Bulk commodities	Light merchandise	13-ton tractor and semi-trailer trucks	8-ton trucks
50	6.53	14.86	5.67	9.76
100	7.35	16.02	9.72	17.12
150	8.18	17.18	13.27	23.22
200	9.00	18.34	16.60	29.56
250	9.83	19.50	19.88	35.35
300	10.65	20.66	22.59	42.16
400	12.36	22.98	29.85	55.77
500	13.95	25.30	37.10	69.38

Source: Government of India, Planning Commission, *Committee on Transport Policy and Coordination: Final Report* (1966), p. 28.
a. Broad gauge only.
b. Road cost estimates for 8-ton trucks are based on the use of roads as they are at present, and those for 13-ton trucks on the use of "good" roads, that is, roads that can carry the much greater loads.

gaining, in which existing transport agencies (including the railways) have the right to protest each application. There are always objections to the issuance of a certificate for trucking over 300 miles. Generally only a temporary certificate is granted, for one month or even for one round trip, with the result that the truck operator wastes endless time renewing licenses.

Financing creates added problems. A truck that costs $5,000 presents a heavy financial burden to Indian operators, but there are no adequate means of obtaining a loan, and finance companies charge as much as 30 percent interest and require payment in 24 months. Large numbers of trucks are regularly repossessed, and there is often a scarcity of buyers, not because there is no need for trucks, but because financing costs add to the probability of unprofitable operations.

Additional burdens result from high taxes and local octroi levies. A truck operating from Delhi to Bombay stops 27 times to pay an average of 100 rupees to various tax collectors en route. Equipment and goods in transit, both representing significant amounts of capital, are stopped one-third of the time during this journey. Further delays are experienced when trucks are held at check points to examine cargo for sales tax enforcement. Truckers must show the origin and destination of each consignment, and its value. Declarations are often double checked by examining the cargo, involving long delays which drivers may avoid by paying the inspector. The resulting costs to the trucking industry are passed on in the form of higher production costs for industry and agriculture.

Despite these delays, truck transport is still much faster than rail (see Table II–5), and it can also be profitable. For example,

TABLE II–5. *Average Time by Rail and Truck between Bombay and Selected Centers*

Center	Average number of hours	
	By rail	By road
Poona	48	8
Baroda	72	45
Ahmedabad	72	65
Nagpur	96	55
Hyderabad	120	65
Madras	192	80
Delhi	192	150
Calcutta	216	180
Satara[a]	144	15
Sangli[a]	168	24
Indore[a]	192	50
Bangalore[a]	192	50
Mysore[a]	240	60

Source: Government of Maharashtra, Finance Department, *Report on Regional Transport Survey of Maharashtra State* (Bombay, 1966), Vol. I, Pt. I: "Report," p. V-81.
a. Involves transshipment at change of rail gauge.

Southern Railways in Madras owns and operates a fleet of trucks and buses in Southern India that provides excellent service and yields a substantial return. Package goods weighing up to 200 pounds are carried at rail rates on reliable schedules, with the help of a large network of company booking offices and agents. Among the principal goods carried are clothing materials, engines, machine tools, tires, household articles, tobacco products, and general merchandise. Although taxes are high, the company is able to finance a retirement fund, education and medical expenses, recreation facilities, bonuses, and other benefits.

Notable in the Southern Railways operations is the emphasis on maintenance and management, with modern workshops that do a general vehicle repair business as well as keep the Southern fleet in condition. Overloading is prohibited, drivers are scientifically trained, and the company policy is to support increased taxes for road improvement. The benefits of this policy can be seen in the large mileage of two-lane roads in Madras State, in the extensive use made of modern road machinery, and in a separate highway department responsible for the road system. Road taxes are used to support the state highway program and to aid local roads, and no local octroi taxes are levied.

The economic advantages of road transport in India are amply demonstrated by the growth and viability of the industry in the face of so many obstacles. But only substantial changes in policy will permit road transport to develop its full potential. Changes of attitude might be fostered by the demonstration effect of a nationwide system of container freight, and by willingness of the railways to operate pickup and delivery truck services and other supplementary trucking operations. These developments can help to relieve the truck operator of the many unnecessary controls that today inhibit efficient transport and raise the cost to consumers.

The current status of long-distance truck transport in India suggests that for some types of traffic moving between major terminals it might be more satisfactory to develop air cargo and integrated air-truck systems. The introduction of planes with very large freight-carrying capacity has upset previous calculations of relative economy. It now appears that, from a total distribution viewpoint, marketing by low-rate but slow surface methods may be more costly than high-rate but fast air transport.

The large jets have a payload of over 40 tons. On the 750-mile Bombay-Delhi air route, their speed of 600 miles/hour would

Modern street in Madras.
Air-India

New jobs in a new industry.

permit three or four round trips per day, compared with perhaps three round trips per month by truck. Thus, while one truck carrying 5 tons each way might generate 22,500 ton-miles per month, a single plane operating 25 days could generate 6,000,-000 ton-miles. In a few years the jumbo jets will be able to provide three times as much transportation as the current models. These developments have particular significance to India, where long distances separate major industrial centers and there are so many obstacles to speedy service on the ground. The higher costs of air cargo might be more than offset by economies realized from changes in plant location, production schedules, inventories, warehousing, and distribution methods.

Integrating Land and Water Transport

The principal task of transport systems development is to coordinate road and rail transport. But integration of land with water transport also has a vital role, mainly involving transfer operations at the ports and the use of coastal shipping as an alternative to land transport.

Coastal shipping has not been a major factor in Indian transport, but the possibilities of fleet modernization and improved port facilities suggest that its role in the movement of coal and other bulk commodities could be much greater. About 4 million tons of dry cargo are transported in coastal ships, nearly half of it coal moving from Calcutta to the ports of Southern India and the Western Coast. Salt is brought to Calcutta on the return trip. Other cargo includes food grains, fertilizer, cement, jute, tea, and iron and steel products. Total dry cargo tonnage has nearly doubled in the past fifteen years, and oil traffic has tripled.

Shipments by water are generally costlier than by rail because most water trips involve two overland movements. Coal, for example, moves overland from the mines to Calcutta, and to reach its final destination usually requires another rail haul.

The distance from East to West Coast ports is also much longer by water than by land (4,700 kilometers by sea from Calcutta to Kandla, compared to 2,400 kilometers by rail). Ships using Calcutta have to travel 126 miles upstream over a dozen sand bars in the Hooghly River to reach port. There are long delays because of waits for favorable tides, and only about two-thirds of the capacity of a 10,000-ton ship can be used in the shallow waters. All of these factors, together with the lack of mechanical loading and unloading equipment, increase the cost of water transport.[9]

The economics of sea transport may be affected importantly, however, by the proposed new port of Haldia, 63 miles below Calcutta. The new facility will reduce the trip upstream from the Indian Ocean from three days to one, and modern handling equipment will further reduce ship turn-around time. It is estimated that the full cost of coal movement by modern 15,000-ton colliers using Haldia will be lower on several routes than the all-rail cost. The journey between the East and West Coasts might be cut 600 kilometers by the proposed canal that would permit ships to pass between Ceylon and India rather than having to round Ceylon.

The economics of both domestic and international water transport depends to a major degree on what is done to improve port efficiency. Beside her 7 major ports, India has 20 intermediate and 150 small ports. The major Indian ports handle about 50 million tons of traffic per year. (See Table II–6.) The persistence of port congestion has had damaging effects throughout the transport system, for delays at the port accentuate shortages of surface transport equipment everywhere. Increased port efficiency depends in part on solving the bulk handling problem. The mixing of bulk and general cargo ships seriously reduces port capacity and creates confusion and high costs in shore operations. It is virtually impossible to coordinate the

---

[9] See Government of India, Planning Commission, *Committee on Transport Policy and Coordination: Final Report*, Chapter VIII.

TABLE II–6. *Traffic Handled by Major Indian Ports, 1964–65*

Ports	Total imports and exports (in millions of tons)	Percent
Bombay	17.3	36
Calcutta	11.1	23
Mormugao	6.6	14
Madras	4.4	9
Visakhapatnam	3.9	8
Cochin	2.8	6
Kandla	2.3	5
Total	48.4	100[a]

Source: Government of India, Planning Commission, *Committee on Transport Policy and Coordination: Final Report* (1966), p. 134.
a. Percents do not total 100 because of rounding.

flow of bulk commodities, which is continuous, with the flow of general cargo, which is erratic.

The successful emergency handling of very large wheat shipments during 1966 indicates that much of the problem in bulk transport could be resolved by mechanizing port operations. Labor-intensive methods have been a costly way of providing jobs. An unloading rate of 1,000 tons of food grains per vessel per day at Calcutta compares with 4,000 tons at Madras and 6,500 tons at Kandla, where there are semi-mechanical unloading facilities.

Productivity could also be substantially raised through the use of containers for general cargo. The amount of cargo worked per hour with the newest general cargo liner is only about ten percent of what can be accomplished with containerized cargo. While a conventional cargo liner may spend three to four days in port, at costs of $3,000 or more per day, containerized ships can load and unload the same cargo in eight to ten hours. Other promising possibilities include all-purpose cargo vessels carrying barges which can be preloaded prior to the ship's arrival in port. By lifting the lighters on and off with a shipboard crane, loading and unloading can be accomplished in shallow water, industrial docks can be served along rivers and

River boats in Kerala.
Air-India

Unloading wheat from ship to rail.

inland waterways, berth congestion is eliminated, and turn-around time cut in half.[10]

Mechanization and the introduction of modern ships can thus assure more effective use of investment in both port facilities and the ships that use them. Since labor costs are low, it will pay to use labor-intensive methods where they can get the same job accomplished in the time that mechanical methods would require. Often this cannot be done, however, and the substitution of labor for capital leads to inefficient use of ships, docks, and surface transport equipment.

India's mounting port traffic calls for further cost-effectiveness studies of new ports and port improvements, such as the Ministry of Transport's study of Haldia. Also needed are forecasts of port traffic on a national basis, and the use of operations research techniques to distribute traffic in accordance with available capacity of both the ports and the connecting land transport lines. The possibility of much greater exports of iron ore and other minerals also suggests the need for coordinated railway-port investments designed to reduce costs and improve India's competitive position in world markets.

Rates and Service

From the viewpoint of an integrated transport system, India's present rate policy has important deficiencies. As in other countries, the period of transport monopoly permitted rates to be based on what the traffic would bear. The charges for moving low-value commodities often consisted only of the costs directly attributable to handling the traffic, with perhaps some contribution toward overhead. High-value commodities, on the other hand, were charged a disproportionate share of common costs

[10] See U.S. Maritime Administration press releases, Feb. 23, 1966, and May 19, 1966.

because the higher rates were insignificant in relation to the final price of the products being moved. In many cases this rate structure persists.

Today the goods on which railways charge high rates are especially vulnerable to road competition. They are often high-value goods moving in small consignments and requiring speedy delivery and careful handling—shipments made to order for the truck. Low-rated commodities, on the other hand, tend to stay on the railways. Railways have the capacity to carry them and to do so cheaply, while trucks are not designed to move large shipments over long distances, and low-rated commodities have no need for fast over-the-road service. The result of traditional pricing policies, then, is for the most remunerative traffic to shift to road, leaving to the rails the traffic that may fail to pay full costs.

The outcome is highly detrimental to the railways. When rates by rail are higher than by road, the inevitable shift from rail to highway creates pressure to provide more highways and trucking. But rail rates that are below cost may also have unfavorable effects by attracting excessive traffic to the railways, creating congestion, and reducing the quality of the service.[11] In many instances the policy may have additional uneconomic effects. Low rates on fuel and raw materials may influence industrial location decisions that ignore the real costs of transportation, thus adding to the nation's total transport bill.

In recent years, steps have been taken to alter the Indian railway rate structure to bring it more into line with costs. Rail charges have been moved upward on bulk commodities such as iron and steel, cement, limestone, ores, salt, and petroleum. Rates have been lowered on tea, rubber, hardware, tobacco, sugar, and biscuits. At the same time, a surcharge of 20 percent levied on "smalls" was extended to somewhat larger shipments

[11] James R. Nelson, "Pricing Transport Services," in Gary Fromm (ed.), *Transport Investment and Economic Development* (Brookings Institution, 1965), p. 218.

because existing rates failed to cover handling costs.[12] These changes in rail rates have been narrowing the gap between costs and prices and have created a sounder basis for road-rail competition.

But the adjustments have not gone far enough, and the obstacles to more realistic pricing are formidable. The objective of maintaining uniformity of railway rates throughout the country often conflicts with the objective of introducing cost-based rates. Uniform rates do not permit high costs on branch lines or meter-gauge routes to be reflected in prices charged, and they deny rail users the savings realized on high-density lines where costs are below average. Nationwide rates also make it impossible to reflect the differences in costs resulting from differences in topography, climate, and railway gauge. The system provides no incentive for regional railway managements to reduce costs, puts the railways at a competitive disadvantage with road transport, and results in an economically unsatisfactory allocation of traffic and investment.

For trucking services the task of rate making is much less a problem. Truck costs are mostly direct costs, since the right of way that is overhead for the rails is paid for largely through taxes collected on a mileage basis. The main problem is that the general level of truck rates is higher than it should be because of taxes, licensing restrictions, financing costs, bad roads, and uneconomic equipment. As a result, the shift from rail to road has been much slower than would otherwise have been the case, thus adding to uneconomic railway operations and investments.

Among the purposes of transport charges are to assure earnings adequate to finance the necessary transport facilities and to provide a return on the investment. "Taken as a whole, the operations of each system of transport . . . should earn at least that rate of return . . . obtained in alternative forms of investment."[13]

---

[12] Details are set forth in "Memorandum Explaining the Proposals for Adjustments in Fares and Freight Rates for Coaching and Goods Traffic, to be effective from 1–4–1966," issued by the Ministry of Railways (1966).

[13] *Committee on Transport Policy and Coordination: Final Report*, pp. 35–36.

Increases in rail rates have not been sufficient to do these things, and have been principally a means of covering increased operating costs. They have not permitted an adequate depreciation fund nor a return on investment comparable to the earnings of other economic activities. In the private sector it has been estimated that rates of return average about 12 percent, whereas the Indian Railways estimated their return at 6.7 percent.[14] Elsewhere it has been estimated that the rate of return on rail investment in the Third Plan was no more than 3.5 to 5 percent.[15]

Since the railways are India's largest business operation, and since the demand for their services has been consistently high, the apparent conclusion is that they should earn enough to finance as much as possible of their investment program internally rather than from general funds. In addition they should be in a position to contribute financially to the development program. These goals suggest the desirability of marketing studies to determine the transportation needs of business and industry, the relation of price changes to demand, and ways of improving rail service and efficiency by adjustments in the demand for transport as well as in the supply. A mutual understanding of carrier potentials and shipper requirements has become necessary to the effective and profitable operations of both participants. The Indian railways have not yet entered the era of selling their services and developing cooperative arrangements with their customers. The growth of road transport is hastening the day.

Accommodating Intercity Travel

Rail freight movement and the policies required to improve it are closely related to passenger traffic that shares the tracks and other facilities. What the future holds for travel, therefore,

[14] Government of India, Ministry of Railways, *Indian Railways, 1963–64*, p. 82.
[15] Louis Lefeber and M. Datta Chandhuri, "Transportation Policy in India," in Paul N. Rosenstein-Rodan (ed.), *Pricing and Fiscal Policy* (Massachusetts Institute of Technology Press, 1964), p. 103.

will be an important influence on freight operations. It will also be a factor in the financial outlook, for the surplus revenue from freight traffic now makes up for the deficit in passenger operations.[16]

Passenger traffic by rail in 1966 was close to 100 billion passenger kilometers—three times the volume of travel on U.S. railways. (See Table II–7.) Travel has been increasing since

TABLE II–7. *Passenger Traffic by Rail and Road, 1950–66*

Year	Passenger volume		
	Rail	Road	Total
	Billion passenger-kilometers		
1950–51	67	23	90
1955–56	62	32	94
1960–61	78	57	135
1965–66	99	85	184
	Percentage		
1950–51	74	26	100
1955–56	66	34	100
1960–61	58	42	100
1965–66	54	46	100
	Index		
1950–51	100	100	100
1955–56	94	136	105
1960–61	117	246	150
1965–66	149	367	204

Source: Government of India, Planning Commission, *Committee on Transport Policy and Coordination: Final Report* (1966), pp. 10, 12; data for 1965–66 supplied by the Planning Commission.

1950 at about the same rate as population. Much of the gain was registered by commuter travel, which more than doubled during the first three plan periods, while intercity traffic increased only a third. (See Appendix Table 11.)

The slower growth of intercity rail trips was primarily the result of bus competition. Bus riding nearly quadrupled be-

[16] See Memorandum by M. R. Bonavia, in Government of India, Planning Commission, *Committee on Transport Policy and Coordination: Final Report*, p. 316.

tween 1950 and 1966, and in the latter year accounted for nearly as much intercity travel as the rails. Bus use increased because on many routes, where light traffic and short trips do not warrant frequent service, the smaller capacity of the bus makes it the most economic method. The shift to bus has been a boon rather than a loss to the railways, for railway passenger service on lightly traveled routes and for short trips is notoriously uneconomic. On 207 lines of meter gauge in Madras State, for example, only 6 percent of passenger operations were able to cover the cost of running the train, and 41 percent covered less than half the operating costs.

Over the longer distances, where speed becomes important, rail travel can be expected to give way to air competition as the system and its equipment are expanded. Indian Airlines Corporation serves 69 cities and towns and increased its patronage from half a million passengers in 1955 to 1.2 million in 1965.[17] (See Appendix Table 12.) But air travel is still concentrated on a small number of routes; only one out of 138 route segments accommodates more than 300 passengers daily, and 76 routes have fewer than 10 riders a day. Thus far, airline travel is little more than one percent of intercity railway traffic.

Transport technology is advancing rapidly, however, and the broad outline of India's emerging pattern of passenger transport suggests the need for many changes, generally in directions already apparent. A more extensive system of high-speed air services will be required for business travel and tourism, while bus lines will have to be extended on lightly traveled routes and to the many communities that are not now served by public carrier. The railways will continue to be the primary carriers on heavily traveled lines.

The charges for passenger travel are the primary determinants of how the Indian people travel today. Fares are lowest

[17] As of 1965, the fleet of Indian Airlines consisted of 4 Caravelles, 12 Viscounts, 10 Fokker Friendships, 3 Skymasters, and 36 Dakotas (Government of India, Planning Commission, *Committee on Transport Policy and Coordination: Final Report*, p. 156).

New mobility by air.

Modern train for commuters.

on ordinary bus and third class rail. From Delhi to Amritsar, for example, a distance of about 300 miles, the bus fare is 12 rupees compared to 14 by third class rail. The trip takes about 11 hours by rail and a half hour longer by bus. The air fare is 95 rupees for the 1 hour 20 minute trip. (See Appendix Table 13.) The fare differential suggests that the 10 hours of time saved by the traveler would have to be worth approximately 80 rupees to make air travel worthwhile for the third class rail traveler. This is 8 rupees per hour, equivalent to more than a dollar at the current exchange rate. The result is that most people travel by bus or rail, and that 97 percent of rail travel is third class.

In the next few years the availability of new jet aircraft with substantially lower seat-mile costs will reduce fares and promote travel. Aircraft operating costs per seat-mile have dropped from 4.6 cents for the DC–3 and 2.5 cents for the DC–6 to an average of 1.3 cents for jet liners.[18] In the near future, the jumbo jets, carrying 500 to 750 passengers, will permit further cost reductions. These developments will make it possible to fly between the principal cities of India for a third of the fare charged today, provided the necessary foreign exchange is available to maintain a modern fleet. In addition, short-haul jets and new vertical take-off and landing craft will be able to increase the number of cities served by air and reduce the costs of airports.

Growth of long-distance bus travel is still inhibited by poor highways and restrictive licensing policies, but the sharp upward trend in bus riding can be expected to continue as these obstacles are gradually overcome. Where the highway network is good, bus transport generally provides the lowest cost passenger service for low density traffic, so that a larger proportion of passenger traffic can be expected to move over the highways in the future.

The indication that in the future all three methods of travel

[18] U.S. Federal Aviation Agency, "Direct Operating Costs and Other Performance Characteristics of Transport Aircraft in Airline Service, Calendar Year 1963" (July 1964), p. 18.

will play a substantial role in passenger transport suggests joint planning of new investments to assure a satisfactory integrated network. Since the major contribution of the railways will continue to be the movement of freight, additional passenger services should not be permitted to interfere with freight operations where bus or air offer an alternative. Branch line rail services should in many cases be discontinued, and the cooperation of the states will be necessary in permitting rail abandonments and in providing alternative bus operations. All extensions of long-distance train service should be evaluated in the light of probable developments in air transport, taking into account that several generations of aircraft will evolve during the service life of most railway equipment. Cost and service comparisons will have to be made between rail technology and tomorrow's aircraft. And new technology may bring other choices; thus, the introduction of high-speed ground transport using guided air cushion systems may prove to be a feasible alternative to air travel for some intercity routes.[19]

The Distribution Revolution

The advances taking place in transportation everywhere have focused attention on the need to achieve an integrated network that will make use of all available technology. Although this requirement is coming to be more generally accepted, it is clear that a broader systems concept needs to be introduced that includes the entire process of production and distribution. What is needed—in India as elsewhere—is not simply the best transport service but the lowest cost method of doing business. There will be many different answers for the varied requirements of Indian industry. For some types of economic activity the best

[19] For the status of new passenger transport technology, see Howard R. Ross, "New Transport Technology," *International Science and Technology*, November 1966, pp. 26–37; and "High-Speed Intercity Ground Transport in 1980," *Journal of the Stanford Research Institute*, No. 12 (November 1966), pp. 2–11.

solutions will be high-cost transport that achieves low-cost distribution. For other industries the situation may differ: higher inventories and greater dependence on warehousing plus less frequent transport may permit lower cost deliveries through full carload or truckload rates. But in all cases the objective will be to deliver to the customer the things he needs when he needs them, at minimum final cost. In some cases this can be accomplished by greater speed and more frequent shipments, and in others by slower transport but faster information exchange.

Assembly lines through which the processes of production have been organized within a plant will in effect have to be extended back to sources of materials and forward to retailer and consumer. Coordination of transport methods themselves is one goal, but there is the further task of adapting transport technology to effective methods of producing and marketing. The potential savings to be realized by this broader systems approach will grow as the volume and complexity of industrial processes increase. This view of transport as an integral part of other economic activities is not restricted to industry, however, for its application is essential to the effective relation between transport and urban design, and between transport and the commercialization of agriculture.

CHAPTER III

Promoting Agriculture and Rural Development

PREOCCUPATION WITH INTERCITY transport dur-
ing the first three Five Year Plans has left local rural transport in
extremely poor condition. The resulting immobility of Indian farmers is one of the principal obstacles to agricultural productivity,
for mobility and accessibility have a part in the total process of
growing and marketing food. It is transport that gets the fertilizer
delivered, that moves the crops to market, and that permits new
ideas to penetrate the villages. Unless the distances that separate ✗
the rural from the urban-industrial economy are bridged, the effort
to increase farm output and to raise rural living standards cannot
succeed.

Eighty percent of India's population lives in 570,000 rural
villages. The majority of these people have no contact with the
outside world. "We never see a stranger," they say when a
stranger finally does appear. They also seldom see the literacy
worker, the agricultural extension agent, or the veterinarian.
One out of three villages is more than five miles from an improved road. The villagers move on foot over tracks scored by
animals, where the going is rough even for the bullocks. This is
the setting in which India seeks in the Fourth Plan to saturate
the farms with fertilizers and to produce 30 million more tons
of food per year.

In the next five years Indian agriculture will not only be
called upon to rebound from the food deficit levels of the mid-

sixties, but to feed the 60 million more people that will swell the population by 1970, and to improve the diet of millions who are now underfed. To do all this it will not be enough to produce the necessary inputs for agriculture, and to help the farmer pay for them and learn how to use them. It will also be necessary to get them where they are needed at the time they are needed. And it will be necessary to provide the market outlets for surplus production and to move produce off the farm to consumers.

Targets for Agriculture

The target for production of food grains by the end of the Fourth Plan is about 120 million tons per year. This means 48 million more tons annually than in the great drought of 1965–66, and 31 million more tons than the record high of 89 million tons in 1964–65. Targets for cotton and jute will be nearly double the volumes currently produced. (See Table III–1.)

TABLE III–1.   *Fourth Plan Targets for Agricultural Inputs and Outputs* (In millions)

Targets	1965–66	1970–71	Percentage increase over 1965–66
Inputs			
Chemical fertilizer (metric tons)	1.6	6.5	306
Irrigation (acres)	24.9	39.0	57
Land reclamation (acres)	4.2	2.5	. . .
Tractors (thousands)	5.6	35.0	525
Outputs			
Food grains (metric tons)	72.3	120.0	66
Cotton (bales)	4.7	8.6	83
Sugar cane (metric tons)	12.1	13.5	12
Oil seeds (metric tons)	6.1	10.7	75
Jute (bales)	4.5	9.0	100

Source: Government of India, Planning Commission, *Fourth Five Year Plan: A Draft Outline* (1966), pp. 62–67.

The impact of this expanded tonnage on transportation will be intensified by two factors. First, the continuing growth of population in urban industrial areas will require moving greater amounts of food long distances to the cities. Second, intensive agriculture will necessitate the movement of a greater volume and variety of products from the urban industrial sector to the farm. If agriculture is to meet the targets set for it, the transportation burden will be much heavier in both directions.

This increase in agricultural inputs is an important new factor affecting transport demand.[1] In the past, when food output could be raised by expanding the area under cultivation, few inputs from the outside were needed. But to achieve higher per-acre yields from land already under cultivation requires the delivery of a variety of inputs. These in turn create agricultural surpluses to be marketed, and their delivery to market enables growers to purchase the next series of inputs.

In this cycle, all-weather roads to Indian villages are a primary requirement. Improved transport can raise per-acre yields by increasing the availability of fertilizers and by making access to the village easier for technicians and agricultural extension workers. Transport improvements have already shifted patterns of agriculture in some parts of India away from less remunerative food grains to vegetables and dairy products. Higher returns to the farmers resulting from this shift have made it possible to purchase increasing amounts of inputs for more scientific agriculture.

Although many factors contribute to agricultural advances, "the use of commercial fertilizer is probably the factor most responsible."[2] Obviously the effectiveness of plant nutrients can be realized only if it is possible to make deliveries on time. For this purpose roads and vehicles have to be provided, along with

[1] Lester R. Brown, "Population Growth, Food Needs and Production Problems," in *World Population and Food Supplies, 1980* (American Society of Agronomy, February 1965), p. 11.

[2] U.N. Food and Agricultural Organisation, *The State of Food and Agriculture, 1963* (Rome, 1963), p. 137.

a network of distribution centers within easy reach of the farmer. Other inputs requiring prompt delivery include pesticides, weed killers and rodent control materials. By 1970–71 the area to be treated with plant protection materials is expected to quadruple, requiring a 167 percent increase in these materials. Total seed delivery will reach a level of 1.3 million tons per year during the Fourth Plan period, and the supply of power-operated and manual equipment for plant protection and irrigation will rise by one-third of a million units to a total of 1.3 million.

The mechanization of agriculture will also require transport to supply the farmer with fuel, lubricants, and spare parts. The number of tractors on Indian farms is increasing noticeably and where roads are adequate, the equipment is also used to haul produce to market. In towns such as Ambala in Haryana and Ludhiana in the Punjab, tractors carrying whole families ride to market with produce loaded in the trailer. Supplies are transported to the farm on the back-haul. In 1960, however, out of a total of 11 million tractors on farms throughout the world, Asia (excluding the Soviet Union) had only 70,000, most of them in Japan.

The use of some types of machinery is desirable even in densely populated areas because it accomplishes two results that could not be achieved by an equivalent use of labor. First, it permits the rapid execution of tasks that nature compels the cultivator to do at specific times. For example, it is necessary to wait until the rains are over before preparing the land for the next crop. If this is done quickly, the land can be used sooner. Thus labor-saving methods are basically time-saving methods that permit better use of the land. The possibility of extending cultivation from one crop per year to double cropping or to nearly continuous cropping increases both output and employment. It also assumes the capability of delivering industrial inputs, including fuel and commercial fertilizers, to make continuous high yields feasible.

The Rural Transport System

India's Fourth Plan targets for agricultural production and the means of achieving them are ambitious indeed when measured against the shortcomings of rural transport. It is estimated that 85 percent of the roads linking villages to the nearest surfaced highway are mere foot tracks unsuitable for vehicle movement. Of the 241,000 miles of village roads and 140,000 miles of district roads, few have any surfacing at all. When the Third Plan got under way, one out of three of India's half a million villages was still more than five miles from a dependable road connection, and 17 percent were more than ten miles distant. (See Table III–2.) Very few Indian farmers more than a mile or a mile

TABLE III–2. *Percentage Distribution of Villages by Distance from an All-Weather Road*

Distance	Percentage of villages
Within village	10.9
Up to 1.5 miles	18.2
Between 1.5 and 3.5 miles	20.7
Between 3.5 and 5.5 miles	12.3
Between 5.5 and 10.5 miles	15.9
Between 10.5 and 20 miles	9.6
More than 20 miles	7.8
Information not available	4.6
Total	100.0

Source: Data are based on a survey undertaken in 1959 by the Ministry of Community Development, Government of India.

and a half from a reasonably good road are using modern methods. Neither farm supplies nor new ideas are moving much beyond that. Since three-fourths of the villages of India are farther than a mile and a half from an all-weather road, it appears that under present conditions transport may limit the possibility of improving the farmer's efficiency to around one quarter of the total farm population.

Wheeled traffic in rural India is principally the bicycle and the bullock cart. An estimated 12 million bullock carts are in operation, the majority used exclusively for agricultural operations. They carry manure, seeds, and seedlings to the fields, and harvested produce to storehouses or to the weekly markets, "which take place regularly at the towns connected by good roads. ..." [3]

The role of the bullock cart has declined with the improvement of roads, and the availability of trucks. It was once common to carry freight up to 50 miles by bullock, but now 25 miles is generally the limit. In addition, the multipurpose bullock is losing his economic justification for transport as electricity and mechanical devices reduce his nontransport uses. Tubewells, tractors, and mechanical threshers release the bullock from water bailing, plowing, and threshing activities. Thus, although these animals have a reputation for furnishing low-cost hauling, increasing mechanization will make this largely an illusion. For when the bullock is viewed as a means of transport alone, his average ton-mile costs may be as high as 20 to 40 cents, while service is no better than 3 miles per hour.[4] In the Kanpur area, case studies have shown that on the average, bullock cart charges paid by cultivators for transporting groundnuts were 5.5 paises per maund (82 pounds) per mile for a 20-mile trip, equivalent to 20 cents per ton-mile. (See Appendix Table 14.)

For the future, shipments of substantial size moving over considerable distances can be transported at reasonable cost only by using motor trucks, and this is not possible where there are no roads or on Indian roads classified as unimproved. Where there is a motorable road, however, and sufficient volume to make use of a truck, it is possible to reduce costs very sharply. For example, when 150 maunds of groundnuts are marketed 50 miles away,

[3] National Council of Applied Economic Research, *Transportation Survey of Madras and Pondicherry* (New Delhi: NCAER, 1965), p. 553.

[4] For details on bullock cart performance, see Government of India, Planning Commission, *Role of Bullock Carts and Trucks in Rural Transport—Case Studies* (1963).

Bullock carts—backbone of traditional transport.

the cost per maund per mile is only 2.1 paises, or about 8 cents per ton-mile. (See Appendix Table 15.)

Transport on village roads presents the worst conditions, but agricultural marketing depends on the total system, and main road transport in a state like Uttar Pradesh, for example, leaves much to be desired. Many state roads are in bad repair. Pontoon or boat bridges, often the only means of river crossing, may be out of operation for as many as four months during the monsoon. The movement of agricultural produce is also handicapped by a trucking radius limited to 150 miles, by the limited number of interstate trucking permits issued, and by numerous bottlenecks in congested towns that further increase transport costs and reduce service. Octroi posts have become a major barrier to efficient road movement. In Shahjahanpur, Basti, Jhansi, Faizabad, and other districts, cash deposits have to be made at import barriers, to be refunded at export barriers, and private agents charge 9 to 15 rupees per truck per entry to provide credit for operators who lack the necessary funds. All these obstacles stand in the way of marketing agricultural output at reasonable returns to the farmer.

The situation is not much better in the more developed state of Maharashtra. Out of 34,361 villages covered during a recent survey of transport, it was found that nearly 27,000 were off the main road system, and that half had no approach roads linking them to the main road. In some parts of the state, three-fourths of the villages off the main roads had no connection, and even among the larger villages with 2,000 people or more, 30 percent had no access roads. Of these villages without connections to the road system, 11,222 were served by cart tracks and 2,231 by foot tracks.[5] (See Table III–3.)

Although Maharashtra has been a pioneer in the establishment of regulated markets, half the 36,000 villages in the state are not near enough to the 226 main market centers and 100 sub-

[5] Government of Maharashtra, Finance Department, *Report on Regional Transport Survey of Maharashtra State* (Bombay, 1966), Vol. I, Pt. II: "Appendices," Tables 6–8.

TABLE III-3.   *Villages without Access to Roads in the State of Maharashtra, 1966*

Category	Number of villages
Villages reporting	34,361[a]
Villages not on main roads	26,947
Villages without approach roads	13,899
Villages connected by cart tracks	11,222
Villages connected by foot tracks	2,231
Villages connected by rivers or other waterways	446

Source: Government of Maharashtra, Finance Department, *Report on Regional Transport Survey of Maharashtra State* (Bombay, 1966), Vol. I, Pt. II: "Appendices," Tables 6 and 8.
a. Out of a total of 35,851 villages surveyed.

yards to be served. For the 17,943 villages that do fall within the jurisdiction of the regulated markets, the average distance to market is nearly 13 miles. Nearly 16 percent are 20 miles away. One-fourth of the villages included in the regulated market areas have only cart tracks to the market place, while another 27 percent are linked partly by village road or main road and partly by foot track or cart track. Only one-fifth of the villages served by regulated markets can reach the market town entirely by surfaced road. A railway station serves 94 of the 226 regulated markets, and another 30 are within ten miles of a railway.

Where no regulated markets are available, wholesale markets serve some villages. There are now 799 villages with wholesale centers—for the most part larger villages, but they represent little over 2 percent of the total. (See Table III-4.)

The Impact of Poor Transport

In areas where transportation is poor, supply problems have severely limited agricultural production. In many areas of the Punjab, the clay surfaces of village access roads become so slippery during two to three months of the monsoon that they cannot be used by pedestrians, let alone animal-drawn carts or bicycles. In these areas it has not been possible to grow vegetables and other perishables for market, since transport must be quick and

TABLE III–4. *Number of Villages and Towns with Wholesale Markets in the State of Maharashtra*

Population group	With market	Without market	Total	Percent with market
0–199	18	6,678	6,696	0.27
200–499	28	10,385	10,413	0.27
500–999	80	10,155	10,235	0.79
1,000–1,999	202	5,756	5,958	3.40
2,000–4,999	281	1,934	2,215	12.69
5,000–9,999	161	144	305	52.70
10,000 and over	29	. . .	29	100.00
Total	799	35,052	35,851	2.28

Source: Government of Maharashtra, Finance Department, *Report on Regional Transport Survey of Maharashtra State* (Bombay, 1966), Vol. I, Pt. II: "Appendices," pp. 1–2.

reliable to enable producers to move their produce to town daily. Even if a poor road is passable, the trip may be too hard on the bullocks. Their principal task is to get the plowing and cultivating done, so that farmers hesitate to tire them by using them for transport.

The attempt to increase milk production is also frustrated when roads are poor. Milk producers living on bad roads find it uneconomical to market their surplus because the milk collector, who travels by bicycle, cannot carry enough on a bad road to make the trip pay. He is able to carry at least twice as much on a good road, and therefore avoids farms with poor access. The only recourse for the isolated farmer is to dispose of his milk locally for whatever he can get.

The return realized by wheat farmers is also limited by the cost of transport over bad roads from village to main highway. This cuts the farmer's margin and prevents him from purchasing the things he needs to run his farm efficiently. He is also unable to specialize, for where transport is unreliable each grower has to produce a little of everything to keep his family supplied. And he retains more than he may actually need, knowing that in the event of a shortage it would be difficult to obtain deliveries from other sources.

The impact of village isolation is documented by a recent study of agricultural conditions in Uttar Pradesh. This state of 90 million people in the Gangetic plain is a farming area of high potential that suffers from low productivity. Wheat production averages only 712 pounds per acre compared to 959 in Punjab State. Rice yields are even more unfavorable: 655 pounds in Uttar Pradesh compared to 827 in Punjab, 970 in Rajasthan, and 1,119 in Andhra Pradesh.

The result is that Uttar Pradesh, where one-third of India's wheat is grown, is a food deficit area despite good soil and the availability of substantial ground water resources. The reasons given for the backward state of agriculture are the absence of sufficient tubewells for irrigation, the short supply of plant nu-trients and other inputs, and the lack of credit facilities. But in early 1967 a report prepared by the state government in Lucknow introduced evidence of still another factor: the extreme difficulty of marketing crops or of obtaining needed inputs in an area where most farmers are miles away from an important market, and often far removed from a road. Fully 36 percent of the vil-lages are without a road, and in hilly areas 50 percent have no road connection.

Road conditions in Uttar Pradesh are an important factor in the lack of tubewells, shortages of fertilizer, backward agricul-tural techniques, and failure to produce more remunerative crops for market. All of these conditions reflect the difficult supply lines to town centers that provide both a market and a source of inputs and technical help. Farmers are not drilling enough tube-wells because accessibility is required to get the drilling equip-ment to the site. Without transport at reasonable cost it is not possible to supply the inputs that modern agriculture requires.

Access to market is not simply a matter of road condition, however, but also of distance to be traveled. For example, of the villages in Uttar Pradesh with no road, 46 percent are 5 to 10 miles from an important market, and 21 percent are more than 10 miles away. Even the 28 percent of villages located on a surfaced road are often remote from market, with fully 11 per-cent more than 10 miles from a major center. These distances are formidable where transport depends on bullock carts, camels, or headloading. But for the other 38 percent of the villages lo-cated on unimproved tracks, the trip to market is even more difficult. (See Appendix Table 16.)

Effects of Transport Improvements

What happens when rural transport is improved has been demonstrated by the village of Wazirpur in Gargaon District, Haryana, where a 12-foot tarred road has brought about sig-nificant changes. Previous to completion of the road, it was pos-sible for the village to obtain cash from the outside only twice a year at the harvest. Now cash is entering the village daily through the sale of vegetables. Vegetables also provide substan-tially larger returns per acre. The new road has also added to village income by increasing the volume of milk sold to neigh-boring towns.

Farmers state that the cost of fertilizer is greatly reduced when it is possible for delivery to be made over a hard-surfaced road. Not only are delivery charges reduced where roads are good; farmers also find it easier to pick up supplies in their own carts. It is also less likely that fertilizer deliveries will be late, which often happens when road conditions are unsatisfactory.

The villagers also reported that it is now possible to conduct high-school classes because teachers are able to ride bicycles from the nearest town. This has permitted women teachers to be em-ployed for the first time. And when roads are improved, the state extends its bus routes to serve the villages, making it possible for girls to attend school in the nearest town. The state picks up all school children free of charge on the state-operated bus network, thus increasing attendance and encouraging consolidated schools. Completion of the road to Wazirpur has also made it possible to establish a dispensary, and to have both doctors and veterinarians available when needed. House construction has also been aided by good roads because the cost of transporting bricks and other materials by truck is one-tenth the cost by camel.

The range of economic and social benefits created by improved rural transport is illustrated by a recent case history.[6] Before construction of the 20-mile Ramnad-Mandapam road in Madras, the towns of Ramnad and Mandapam were joined by rail and by a narrow path, unusable even as a cart track. Mechanized road transport was totally absent. After the new road was opened, two bus companies began operations. Regional milling and pottery industries were established, the fishing industry expanded, and many retail shops were opened. In addition, a network of feeder roads partly induced by the new highway has brought nearby village prices more in line with those prevailing in the Ramnad market. The number of elementary schools and student enrollment have increased, six post offices are operating compared with three before the road was built, and a number of dispensaries have been built.

The situation is duplicated in many parts of India. In one village in Rajasthan the construction of a five-mile hard-surfaced link road changed the whole pattern of farm life. There was an increase in tubewell construction, which permitted sugar cane to be grown and transported to the mill. A cooperative society was started for the supply of fertilizer, and new developments included a hospital, two new schools, and four bus lines with connections to Delhi.

Linking Transport to Intensive Agriculture

The evidence suggests that among the prerequisites of rural development are greater reliability of transport and reduced transport costs. The question, however, is how to design an effec-

[6] Government of India, Ministry of Transport and Communication, Department of Transport (Roads Wing), *Economic Benefits of the Ramnad-Mandapam Road, 1959–60* (1961).

tive attack on rural transport deficiencies. One indication of India's road needs is the ratio of miles of road per square mile of cultivated area on the subcontinent compared to the ratio in other parts of the world. In agriculturally advanced Western countries, the number of miles of farm-to-market roads per square mile of cultivated land varies between 3 to 1 and 4 to 1. The lower ratio is found mainly in grain-producing areas where fields are large; the ratio rises where farms are smaller and the topography difficult. In Britain, France, Japan, and the United States, the ratio is around 4 to 1. In Taiwan and Denmark it is closer to 3 to 1. In Malaya it is about ¾ to 1, and in the Philippines around 1 to 1. In India the ratio is only about ⅔ of a mile of road to 1 square mile of cultivated land.

The statistics indicate that a certain minimum density of farm-to-market roads is present where rural development has achieved high levels, and that none of the poor countries has nearly enough mileage.[7] Applying these figures to India, where about half a million square miles are farmed, a conservative ratio of two miles of road per square mile of cultivated land area would call for a million miles of road. There are now around 600,000 miles, about 177,000 of them with some type of surfacing. An additional 400,000 miles would have to be constructed if the ratio of mileage to cultivated acreage were to be comparable to half the density found in France or Britain. However, most of the existing rural network is in extremely poor condition, so that the task of upgrading this mileage is equally urgent.

A program of this magnitude highlights the importance of concentrating efforts mainly on the potential payoff from improved agriculture rather than permitting political and geographic considerations to govern. In the past, the objective of the road-building effort has been to bring every village in a developed agricultural area within 4 miles of a metalled road and 1.5 miles

[7] Edgar L. Owens, "Development through Democratic Institutions" (unpublished manuscript, 1965).

of some road by 1981.[8] Other villages were to be brought within 8 to 12 miles of a surfaced road, or 3 to 5 miles of an unsurfaced road. The weakness of this program has been the absence of economic criteria; that is, the lack of any relation to the goal of increasing agricultural output. The opportunity to promote India's agricultural efforts by relating the road program specifically to the food problem has not been exploited.

Current efforts at intensive cultivation offer a new opportunity to focus local road improvements on the goal of achieving higher agricultural yields. The initial effort of this kind was the Intensive Agricultural District Program (IADP), undertaken to concentrate needed agricultural inputs in certain areas having good soil and other conditions favorable to production. This "package program" was designed to provide the means of realizing an area's potential. The means include help to individual farmers in soil preparation, water management, and the application of fertilizers, seed, pesticides, tools, power sprayers, dusters, and other farm machinery. The IADP also provides a variety of "off-the-farm" services essential to increased productivity, including training, credit, cooperatives, and storage.

As could be expected, the areas where intensive efforts have been actually undertaken are those in which transport was good enough to permit the inputs to be moved and the output to be marketed. The Ludhiana District of the Punjab, one of these areas, has a main road net that assures all-weather access. There the package program led to marked increases in wheat production per acre.[9] After three years of the five-year experiment the yield per acre had increased 40 percent, the area under cultivation had grown, and total output had expanded 68 percent. The consumption of chemical fertilizers increased five-fold in three years.[10]

[8] Government of India, Ministry of Transport and Communication, Department of Transport, *Report of Chief Engineers on Road Development Plans for India, 1961–81* (1958), p. 32.

[9] Ludhiana District has 800,000 acres and 1.2 million people. It is about 40 miles by 20 miles. In each of the ten blocks of the District, there are 80 villages.

[10] See Intensive Agricultural District Program, Ludhiana, "Story of Wheat, Groundnut and Maize in Ludhiana" (mimeographed, 1964).

As a result of these efforts, farmers in Ludhiana District were getting an additional return of 126 rupees per acre compared to extra costs of 54 rupees, a net gain of 72 rupees. Experience was equally gratifying in Orissa, where rice yields averaged 2,500 pounds per acre in the package districts compared to 1,700 pounds elsewhere. The additional return per acre was 110 rupees, compared to incremental costs of 60 rupees.[11]

The intensive agricultural approach initiated by the IADP was later extended to 160 Intensive Agricultural Areas (IAA) throughout the country. These are areas that specialize in specific types of production such as rice or millet, but the IAA program is designed to increase whatever additional crops are grown in the area. The IAA program covers 20 to 25 percent of all cultivated land in India.[12] In 1967 special efforts were being made on some 32 million acres within these areas to carry out a new high-yield varieties program where conditions are especially suited to maximum production.

It is in these agricultural areas marked for special treatment that transport investments should be concentrated if they are to contribute most to the development effort. The importance of orienting the transport program to agriculture is emphasized by the fact that improved transport is likely to have disappointing results without the other conditions that need to be present to activate economic growth. Where farmers are willing to participate in the intensive programs and where the needed inputs are available, transport can act as the catalyst for improved agriculture. A "prior dynamism" must be present to assure that investment in transport will pay off.[13] The transport program should thus be designed to support areas of latent growth potential, where the soil, the amount of assured water, and the intention

[11] Ford Foundation, "India's Intensive Agricultural District Program," India Program Letter 134 (mimeographed; New Delhi, July 10, 1964).

[12] See M. S. Randhawa, *Intensive Cultivation Programmes* (Government of India, Ministry of Food and Agriculture, 1965).

[13] George W. Wilson, Barbara R. Bergmann, Leon V. Hirsch, and Martin S. Klein, *The Impact of Highway Investment on Development* (Brookings Institution, 1966).

to expand the use of agricultural inputs provide the guarantee of a good return on the combined investment.

To illustrate, a 10-mile stretch of road that is surfaced to make possible intensive agriculture can be expected to influence the surrounding land to a depth of at least one mile from the roadway. Thus a total of 10 square miles on each side of the road, 20 square miles in all, will be opened up for intensive cultivation, or a total of 12,800 acres. Based on the experience of the Intensive Agricultural District Program, this land can be assumed to be yielding an average of 1,000 pounds of wheat per acre prior to intensive cultivation, of which 20 percent, or 200 pounds per acre, is marketed. The total marketed surplus for the entire 12,800 acres is thus 2.5 million pounds. With the opening of the road, however, it becomes possible to use substantial amounts of fertilizers and other inputs. On the basis of IADP experience, output should double to 2,000 pounds per acre. If it is assumed that all of the additional 1,000 pounds of output are sold, the marketable surplus is increased by 10.3 million pounds. The extra costs incurred to obtain the increased yield during the first year are listed in Table III–5.

The cost figure of 4.1 million rupees shown in the table is based on charging all of the new road cost to the first year of

TABLE III–5.   *Cost of Doubling Per Acre Yield of Wheat*
(In rupees)

Items in cost	Per acre	Total for 12,800 acres
Fertilizer	120	1,536,000
Seed	50	640,000
Irrigation	110	1,408,000
Plant protection	15	192,000
Road construction (10 miles)	24	300,000
Road maintenance	3	30,000
Cost of carting	2	23,000
Total extra cost per acre	325	4,129,000

Sources: Input costs are from Kanpur Agricultural College, Uttar Pradesh. Road costs are based on a Ministry of Transport estimate of Rs. 30,000 per mile, with 10 percent for maintenance. Transport cost is based on the assumption of 3 paises per maund-mile for marketing by bullock cart. Truck costs would be lower.

the program. If road cost is allocated over an assumed 10-year life, annual capital cost with 20 percent interest would be only about 33,000 rupees per year, and total input costs would be reduced to 3.86 million rupees. The increased income realized from the extra 12.8 million pounds of wheat would be substantially greater. If the market price of wheat is one-third of a rupee per pound, total value of the extra crop would be close to 4.3 million rupees. Return on the investment is about 12 percent.

Additional benefits would accrue from the reduction in transport costs for the 200 pounds of marketable surplus per acre that previously moved over the poor road, and is now transported over the improved road. Transport costs by bullock cart are reduced from 5 to 3 paises per maund-mile when a dirt road is surfaced with stone or gravel. The savings from reduced transport costs would amount to 3,040 rupees per year for the area served by the 10-mile road, assuming that the surplus of 2.5 million pounds previously realized through the old methods of production will move an average of 5 miles over the improved 10-mile road section en route to market. Additional savings not included here would result from cheaper transportation of those inputs employed in the area prior to road improvement and more intensive cultivation.

Further advantages result from the changes in village life that follow construction of an all-weather road, such as the improvement of the school, better school attendance, and greater availability of medical and veterinary services. And in a nation with a large food deficit and an unfavorable balance of payments, a primary advantage is the reduction of foreign exchange costs for food imports.

When the ingredients of an intensive agricultural effort are measured in cost per acre, the outlay required to build a satisfactory access road is a relatively small part of the total. Even assuming that the road is to be paid for entirely during the first year, road cost per acre, as shown in Table III–5, is less than half the cost of improved seed, and total costs for road construction and maintenance are less than 10 percent of the intensive cultivation program. And if road costs are allocated over the life of the road, cost per acre is further reduced in relation to the total. Thus even if the outlays for road construction should be doubled to meet difficult soil and monsoon conditions, they would still be modest per acre.

Financial Obstacles

If the road is such an important and relatively inexpensive ingredient of intensive cultivation, why are not more villages involved in road improvement programs? One answer is that financing arrangements are extremely difficult. In Haryana, villages that agree to pay one-fourth the cost of access roads are provided with the other three-fourths by the Public Works Department. To date, only 20 of the 400 villages in the District have pledged funds to be matched by the state. Matching can be either in labor or in money. In many cases, however, villagers are too poor to afford the taxes required to permit a cash contribution. In addition, it is frequently not possible for farm workers to spend any time on roadbuilding; all their time is needed to earn a living on the farm.

The cost of a 12-foot road with 4 inches of stone or gravel averages about 50,000 rupees per mile, including tarring. This amounts to 20 to 25 rupees per head for most villages that wish to contribute in cash, but if the road is longer than average, it may require 40 to 50 rupees per head. If the payment is made in kind and work is done over an 8 to 9-hour day, it generally involves about 10 days of work to make the local contribution in labor instead of taxes. The labor is used for earth work, valued at the rate of about 3 rupees per day, and is supervised by the Public Works Department.

These factors help to explain why so few villages are participating in the road program. But even for these villages the program has not been able to move ahead; the Public Works Department lacks funds to match the monies committed locally, because many main roads in very poor condition demand priority.

If an accelerated local road program were to be undertaken, how much would it cost, and how would it be paid for? Costs would depend on the varying requirements of different parts of the country. For example, the Punjab has a good network of main highways, but poor village approach and connecting roads. Particular difficulties occur in the monsoon, when most of the village road network becomes impassable. In Rajasthan, on the other hand, sandy soil and a relatively dry climate permit any village to be reached by jeep at any time without expensive road construction. Even in the rainy season the drainage is so good that most roads actually improve in quality. But there is a dearth of major district roads in the area, and these more costly long-distance routes, rather than the shorter village access roads, are the highest priority needs. Better access roads will be required at a later date, after the availability of electric power for irrigation systems enables dry lands to produce enough surplus to warrant truck transport.

Road requirements and road costs are thus subject to widely differing conditions. Data from various parts of the country, however, indicate that all-weather access roads in much of India can be built for an average of $4,000 per mile. In some areas of good sandy soil, and with plentiful stone and gravel near at hand, it will be possible to reduce the figure. But where rainfall is heavy, more bridges and culverts raise the cost, and blacktopping is often necessary. Also, the fact that some of the required farm-to-market roads are district highways rather than approach roads adds to the outlay. However, the average figure of $4,000, or 30,000 rupees, per mile cited by the Ministry of Transport can be expected to take most of these differences into account.

As already indicated, a million-mile network of road appears to be a minimum need for all of India, based on relations between road mileage and cultivated area around the world. About 421,000 miles of unimproved rural access roads are already laid out but in need of major improvement. It is assumed that one-fifth of this existing rural network, or 84,000 miles, is in the one-fifth of India encompassed by the Intensive Agricultural Areas and would be included in a road program to support the intensive cultivation program. Additional mileage would then need to be added to serve the many villages without roads.

How much of the existing mileage needs to be improved beyond grading and drainage will depend on local conditions, but experience with getting the farmers of the United States out of the mud in earlier years provides some interesting and fairly relevant information.[14] In 1949 the United States had 2.5 million miles of local rural roads. Yet despite the high degree of mechanization and motorization of America's farms, more than half this local road network was still unsurfaced, and 90 percent of the surfaced mileage was gravel. Where there were fewer than 10 to 25 vehicles a day, it was found uneconomic to provide a dustless surface. Generally, traffic of 50 to 100 vehicles a day was required before a granular surface was black-topped. The most significant continuing uses of local roads were as routes for mail service (1.5 million miles), school buses (700,000 miles), and milk collections (500,000 miles).

Of all American farms in 1945, 64 percent were on an all-weather road; 10 percent were less than a mile distant, 21 percent were from 1 to 5 miles, and 4 percent over 5 miles. (Among the modern conveniences found on farms at that time, the most widespread was radio. Only 25 percent of farms had running water, and 20 percent had trucks, but 75 percent had radios).[15]

The cost of building local rural roads naturally varied with climate, topography, and road design. Roads that were graded and drained on adequate alignment and surfaced with 3 inches of gravel cost approximately $3,500 per mile for a 10-foot width, and annual maintenance costs were about $150 per mile. On the average it cost about $6,000 per mile for gravel roads of all

[14] See U.S. Department of Commerce, Bureau of Public Roads, *The Local Rural Road Problem* (January 1950).

[15] See Chapter V for a discussion of the role of radio in rural India and other countries.

types throughout the country. For the system as a whole, half the annual expenditures on roads was for maintenance.[16]

Of additional significance to India, embarking for the first time on a local road program of major dimensions, is the finding that a substantial percentage of local roads built in the United States up to 1950 rendered "little or no service of any kind." In Vermont, 24 percent of all local mileage was in this category. For Oregon the figure was 17 percent. Altogether, according to the Bureau of Public Roads estimate, 400,000 miles of American local roads proved to be nonessential. At an average cost of $6,000 per mile, the overbuilding of rural roads cost the United States $2.4 billion.

In the light of this experience, it is probable that of both new and existing roads in the Intensive Agricultural Areas a substantial percentage can be left unsurfaced, and relatively few roads need a surface of either gravel or blacktop. The major task will be grading and drainage. If specific project analyses indicate need for about twice as much total mileage as now exists, work would thus be required on about 168,000 miles of road to support IAA efforts throughout the country. With a weighted average for both surfaced and unsurfaced roads of $4,000 per mile, total costs would be $672 million.

Many local roads in other areas will also need to be improved, but it would appear to be prudent public policy to concentrate in the Fourth Plan on the roads that are needed to serve intensive cultivation programs. Where roads outside these areas are clearly needed for the production of food, and state help is requested, projects should be considered on their merits.

Other Requirements and Prospects

Improved transport requires vehicles as well as roads, and improved marketing requires storage facilities, processing, and the

[16] U.S. Department of Commerce, Bureau of Public Roads, *The Local Rural Road Problem*, p. 43.

necessary institutions for financing and delivering inputs and for selling what is grown.

The cooperative movement has made some advances in the marketing of agricultural produce, especially such commodities as cotton, tea, and sugar. A total of 57 cooperatives serve over a million and a half sugar cane growers and account for one-fourth of the industry's processing capacity. Some cooperatives do not engage in marketing activities, but sell farm supplies only. Altogether, cooperative sales amounted to one-third of all the fertilizers used in India in 1960, and the proportion of their sales has been increasing.

The growing importance of agricultural inputs, the problems of getting them delivered on time, and the increased output moving to market suggest that providing farm transport services should be one of the functions of regulated markets and cooperatives. As road conditions improve, these organizations could operate trucks for the delivery of supplies and consumer goods, and for the collection of produce for sale, including milk and dairy products, fruits, vegetables, and food grains.

Agricultural products containing high protein are generally quite perishable, especially in heat and humidity, and a large proportion of the world's food grain is lost because storage is either unavailable or inadequate.[17] Scientifically designed storage capacity of the right size and in the right location is a further requirement if what is produced is to be protected from the weather and from disease and infestation. Adequate storage capacity makes it possible to hold on to supplies until market conditions are favorable, rather than selling at the harvest when prices are lowest. Storage space also makes it possible to consolidate the small output of individual farmers to improve sales opportunities. Greater reliance on storage of agricultural products close to the source provides the added advantage of reducing the congestion on the railways which results from attempting to move the entire crop at once.

[17] U.N. Food and Agricultural Organisation, *The State of Food and Agriculture, 1964* (Rome, 1964), p. 125.

Processing, along with storage, can play a major supporting role in marketing. A recent estimate indicates that one-fourth to one-third of all the fruit and vegetable production of India is lost through poor handling.[18] Much of this loss occurs in transit. Processing not only helps to protect and preserve food, but permits a substantial loss of extraneous weight at the source and therefore a saving in the tonnage that needs to be hauled. Other benefits include the creation of local employment and income from the value added to agricultural output by processing.

Changes in agricultural patterns made possible by improved transport can also play a larger role in relieving food shortages. Most of India's protein requirements are now derived from grains. But protein supplies could be substantially increased by expanding vegetable and fruit production, provided transport problems can be overcome. Fruits and vegetables now constitute only 3 percent of world protein sources, yet one hectare of leafy green vegetables can produce four times as much protein as the same plot of land sown as pasture to feed cows for the production of milk. The supply of proteins plus vitamins and minerals could also be enlarged by producing more beans, peas, and lentils, which contain three to four times as much protein as grains. These pulse crops also add to the productivity of the soil. Greater use of these foods would be possible with improvements in marketing and transportation.

Food from the sea is another important source of human sustenance that could be further exploited. Only 3 percent of the protein consumed by the world's population comes from the oceans. Improved transport has encouraged the marketing of fish in India, but the requirements for speed and refrigeration involve high costs. Of much greater promise is the processing of fish products that can be stored and then transported.

In the long run, science may provide some exotic solutions to the food problems of India. For example, the amount of protein

[18] U.S. Department of Agriculture, Economic Research Service, *Changes in Agriculture in 26 Developing Nations 1948–63*, Foreign Agricultural Economic Report No. 27 (1965), p. 109.

currently supplied by all the world's animals could be produced from a very small fraction of the world's annual output of petroleum, and there are vast amounts of nutrition available in plants and grasses everywhere. These do not appear to be exploitable food sources during the next 15 to 20 years, however. The main reliance will be on scientific application of fertilizers and the introduction of improved seed, together with increased farm mechanization, storage facilities, and food processing, plus changes in the kinds of crops grown.[19]

These steps toward the commercialization of agriculture all require the development of readily accessible markets where inputs can be purchased and where produce can be assembled for processing and sale. What is needed is an extension of the regulated market to meet all the needs of the farmer in the campaign to raise more food. Regulated markets, now limited to the handling of food grains and cotton, have been authorized by state legislation in more than half of India's states. They have flourished particularly in cotton-growing areas, but their services are needed by all agricultural producers. Regulated markets are operated under public supervision by boards composed of producers and buyers. Their functions include providing the necessary physical facilities for traders, such as overnight accommodations, water supply, display space, and warehousing. In addition, produce is graded at the market, weighing is supervised, and fair prices are paid. These activities are supplemented by retail establishments selling consumer goods and agricultural supplies, and by banking and credit facilities.[20]

To date the coverage provided by regulated markets is grossly inadequate. There is only one such market for every 6,766 villages in Bihar, and only one per 4,030 villages in Rajasthan. If India were to aim for a minimum of one regulated market for every 100 villages there would need to be several thousand of

---

[19] Howard W. Mattson, "Food for the World," *International Science and Technology,* December 1965, pp. 28–39, 95–96.

[20] See National Council of Applied Economic Research, *Market Towns and the Spatial Economy of India* (New Delhi: NCAER, 1965).

these major market facilities. In addition to the large regulated market, however, there is need throughout India for smaller market towns which can serve as subassembly points easily available to all farmers.[21] The location of these regulated markets and submarkets should be guided by the transport potentials of trucks and better roads, and their location in turn would provide a basis for selecting the access routes to be improved.

Transport Strategy for Agriculture

A broader strategy is needed, then, to guide transport and related agricultural planning as part of a total plan for rural development. If the resources available to improve agriculture are to be employed to maximum advantage, it is necessary to weigh the merits of various combinations of inputs. Public policy makers should avoid overemphasizing transportation to the neglect of the combination of roads, vehicles, storage, and processing solutions that together will bring the highest return to farmers.

Instead of planning transport in isolation, a systems approach to agricultural development is essential to link transport policy with the goals that transport is called upon to serve—in this case to increase the production and marketing of food. Success will call for the close collaboration of transport and agriculture officials at both national and local levels. A basic requirement will be flexibility in plans and in the use of development funds.

A combined agriculture and transport program for food production, together with related investments, would include, in sum:

1. Cooperatives or regulated markets providing for (a) the distribution of fertilizer, seed, insecticides, and tools and the rental of tractors and other equipment; (b) loans for the purchase of agricultural inputs, payable through the delivery of produce for marketing; (c) the sale of consumer goods; (d) the operation of trucks for pickup and delivery service.

[21] Further discussion of the new towns needed for both agriculture and industry is contained in Chapter IV.

2. A network of storage facilities to minimize loss of crops and to reduce the peak flow of perishables at the harvest.

3. The establishment of food processing plants to meet the needs of urban markets and to provide local employment and income.

4. A network of roads in areas of superior agricultural potentials, located to provide transport from the villages to market centers, with construction and maintenance providing local employment and fostering the improvement of local administration services.

A systems approach to transport and agriculture, then, leads away from building transport for the sake of transport, and instead concentrates on the objectives of agricultural production and rural development. Investments need to be programmed as part of a package of things that separately may have limited impact, but in combination may produce the food that is essential to India's survival.

CHAPTER IV

Transport and the
New Urban Geography

WHILE THE ISOLATION resulting from poor trans-
port has been a principal obstacle to rural development and to
agriculture, mounting congestion has become a growing threat to
the viability of large urban centers. Population growth, migration,
and the concentration of economic activity in Calcutta, Delhi,
Bombay, and other major cities have created urban problems of
every kind. These centers are suffering from shortages of housing,
water and sanitary facilities, from high rates of unemployment and
disease, and from a lack of every kind of amenity. Transport facilities are being overwhelmed by the crush of people traveling
between home and work, and by the tangle of goods traffic that
somehow keeps the cities alive and functioning. These problems
have reached staggering dimensions even before the tidal wave of
rural to urban migration has reached its peak.

Two types of remedies are called for. One is the development
of a national pattern of urban settlement which takes advantage of the wider locational choices made possible by road and
air transport. Previously it was necessary to continue to concentrate urban growth in high-density areas; the location of
cities was dictated by existing limited capabilities of water and
rail transport, and by the difficulties of communication. Today
changes in transport and telecommunications introduce greater
flexibility in the location and design of cities. These new technologies offer hope for a more satisfactory setting for urban

Motor traffic in Bombay.
Air-India

industrial development in India. An equally important remedy, for both old and new cities, is a combination of improved transport systems and land use planning that lightens the burdens of city transport. Reducing transport requirements through new solutions to problems of urban design may help to release resources for the more pressing problems of providing potable water, sewerage systems, and shelter.

Urban Trends and Underlying Causes

Only one-fifth of India's population lives in cities, while in many industrialized countries the proportion is often four-fifths or higher. The proportion of urban dwellers in India is bound to grow larger, however, as population increases and as the migration from rural areas is accelerated by the declining availability of jobs in agriculture. It is estimated that in the year 2000 a third of India's people will be living in urban places, 125 million more than today.[1]

The great majority of India's people live in rural villages. Over one-third of a million villages have fewer than 500 people, another hundred thousand have between 500 and 1,000. (See Table IV–1.) At the other end of the scale are 248 cities, each with more than 50,000 inhabitants. Three of these, Calcutta, Delhi, and Bombay, are among the twenty-five largest metropolitan centers in the world. (See Table IV–2.) Calcutta is the world's tenth largest city, with nearly 6 million people. Bombay is eleventh with 4.2 million, and Delhi is twenty-fourth, with 2.3 million. Between 1941 and 1961, population growth was 237 percent in Delhi, 145 percent in Bombay, 144 percent in Bangalore, 69 percent in Hyderabad, and 57 percent in Calcutta.[2] Growth rates have been greatest in the major centers,

[1] A. J. Coale and E. M. Hoover, *Population Growth and Economic Development in Low Income Countries* (Princeton University Press, 1958), App. A, Table A–9.

[2] See Kingsley Davis, "Urbanization in India: Past and Future," in Roy Turner (ed.), *India's Urban Future* (University of California Press, 1962), p. 10.

Congestion at Old Delhi's "Moonlight Crossing."
John Scofield © 1963 National Geographic Society

rising 48 percent in the 107 cities of 100,000 population and over, and only 21 percent in cities of 10,000 to 20,000. (See Table IV–3.)

High and low projections for the year 2000 present a very wide range of figures. For Calcutta the low estimate is 36 million and the high 66 million. Delhi might have 18 million inhabitants or as many as 33 million. But whatever credence one gives to these estimates, it is clear that finding effective measures to prevent the growth of unmanageable super-cities poses a most urgent current challenge for Indian economic planning.

TABLE IV–1. *Indian Population Centers: Distribution by Size*[a]

Size[b]	Number of cities and villages
Over 50,000	248
20,001–50,000	398
10,001–20,000	853
5,001–10,000	3,081
2,001–5,000	20,374
1,001–2,000	51,478
501–1,000	103,639
Under 500	367,027

Source: National Council of Applied Economic Research, *Market Towns and Spatial Development in India* (New Delhi: NCAER, 1965), p. 117.
a. India is comprised of 18 states, 320 districts, and 5,200 blocks.
b. As of March 31, 1962.

Several causes underlie the trends that are crowding Indians into hopelessly congested urban slums. One has been the millions of refugees who fled to India following partition of the subcontinent. They have added to the staggering burdens of the largest cities, and their impact has not yet been fully absorbed. This influx has magnified the task of providing shelter, jobs, and minimum standards of public service.

The lack of opportunity in rural villages and in agriculture is another reason for migration to the cities. The rate of economic progress in the cities, however, has not been sufficient to absorb this in-migration plus the natural population increase. Here, the underlying problem is the addition of 12 million people

Horse-drawn tongas vying with other traffic.
John Scofield © 1963 National Geographic Society

annually to India's total population. As a result, urban unemployment accounts for half of the nation's total unemployment—and nearly half of India's educated unemployed are concentrated in the four largest cities.[3] In addition, millions find only marginal employment in trade and services, so that the phenomenon of rural underemployment is duplicated, often under worse conditions, in the big cities.

TABLE IV–2. *Population of Major Indian Cities in 1961 and Projections for the Year 2000*
(In millions)

Metropolis[a]	Population, 1961	Projections, 2000[b]	
		Low	High
Greater Calcutta	5.6	35.6	66.0
Delhi	2.3	17.8	33.0
Greater Bombay	4.2	11.9	22.0
Madras	1.7	8.9	16.5
Bangalore	0.9	7.1	13.2
Ahmedabad	1.2	5.9	11.0
Hyderabad	1.1	5.1	9.4
Kanpur	0.9	4.5	8.3
Poona	0.6	4.0	7.3
Nagpur	0.6	3.6	6.6

Sources: Data for 1961 for all but Calcutta, Delhi, and Bombay are from S. H. Steinberg (ed.), *The Statesman's Yearbook, 1963–64* (St. Martin's Press, 1963), p. 422; all other data are from Kingsley Davis, "Urbanization in India: Past and Future," in Roy Turner (ed.), *India's Urban Future* (University of California, 1962), pp. 10, 25.
a. Ranked according to their relative position in the year 2000.
b. For a detailed discussion of the methods of obtaining these projections, see Davis, "Urbanization in India."

The reasons why people migrate to the city were examined in a survey of industrial workers in Kanpur. Population pressure on the land and the economic difficulties of supporting a large family were the most important factors. A few people cited reasons such as family disputes and caste difficulties, but economic factors were predominant.[4]

Of those who came to the city for employment, 46 percent got a job immediately after arrival, and another 13 percent

[3] Wilfred Malenbaum, "Urban Unemployment in India," *Pacific Affairs*, June 5, 1957, pp. 138–50.
[4] Information from an untitled paper by G. P. Goyal and A. K. Srivastava, presented at the International Seminar on Industrial and Urban Growth of Kanpur Region, Kanpur, India, Jan. 29–Feb. 4, 1967.

were employed within a month. But for 15 percent it was more than a year after migration before the first job was obtained. Moreover, the job a person must take on first arrival is generally not to his liking and pays poorly. Newly-arrived workers usually lack the resources that might permit them to be unemployed for any length of time, but the possibility of being jobless is always a threat. Thus, among industrial employees in Kanpur during a given year, 33 percent were without work for over three months, 18 percent for two to three months, and 21 percent were idle one to two months.

TABLE IV–3.   *Growth of Urban Places in India, 1951–61*

Size	Number of places		Population (in millions)		Increase in population (in percent)
	1951	1961	1951	1961	
Class I (100,000 and over)	74	107	24	35	48
Class II (50,000–100,000)	111	141	8	10	28
Class III (20,000–50,000)	375	515	11	16	41
Class IV (10,000–20,000)	670	817	9	11	21

Source: Table is based on data from the U.S. Agency for International Development.

Despite the problems revealed by the Kanpur survey, the cities hold a strong attraction for the villager, who is influenced to migrate not only because of the unsatisfactory conditions in his rural surroundings but because of the pull exerted by potential economic and social opportunities in an urban center. Four-fifths of the migrant workers interviewed in Kanpur felt that the city had better opportunities for employment and economic advancement. In addition, 40 percent mentioned the availability of recreation in the city, such as shows, movies, parks, sports, games, and exhibitions. The opportunity to give children an education was mentioned by half of all respondents as one of the factors inducing migration to the city. Yet there was also widespread dissatisfaction with urban living. The major complaint, scarcity of food, was cited by 61 percent of the migrating workers. Lack of housing was mentioned by 37 percent, and unsanitary conditions by 52 percent.[5]

‑ Personal reasons for the trend toward the city are reinforced by a number of geographic, historical, and technological reasons. In India the shortage of good natural harbors has limited the number of port cities and has caused Calcutta, Bombay, and Madras to become the focal points of industries that rely on cheap ocean transport. Each city has also developed ties with an extensive hinterland, from which it attracts large numbers of people.

Once the urbanization process has begun, it is self-perpetuating. Industry thrives on a large labor supply, extensive local markets, and the complementary nature of many business activities. Individual plants need to be of sufficient size to permit the economies of large-scale production, and in India there is a definite need for plants of larger capacity to reap these economies.[6] A city itself needs a sufficient number of plants to make possible the economic use of its power and other utilities and services, and a sufficient number of people to support the variety of institutions that are the rewards of urban living. Economic activities are attracted to where transport and other supporting facilities already exist, regardless of their inadequacies. The social costs of more crowding are borne, not by the newcomers, but by everyone living and working in the big city. Thus the burden of over-concentration is diffused, and the economic calculations of individual decision makers fail to check the trends.

Congestion and Its Costs

Limited information about the relation between city size and cost per capita of necessary accommodations indicates that big city living is expensive. Indian data show that per capita mu-

[5] *Ibid.*

[6] Alan S. Manne, "Plant Size, Location and Time-Phasing" (unpublished manuscript, Stanford University, 1966).

nicipal expenditures in a city of 132,000 were 10 rupees, compared to 40 rupees in Bombay, exclusive of independent public corporations. Public housing costs in Bombay were two to three times as much as in the smaller city.[7]

In the big city the cost of shelter makes it impossible for most people to afford satisfactory accommodations. High-density tenements cost two to three times as much as ordinary one-story houses because they require modern materials and technology, as well as skilled labor and supervision. The rent of a dwelling may be $20 per month. If it is assumed that one-fifth of a worker's wages will be spent for housing, to afford this level of shelter a family needs an annual income of $100 per month. But only 12 percent of the urban population earns as much as half this amount, and the average income is less than $100 for an entire year.[8] These figures explain the colonies of squatters who take over public and private lands wherever they can for their shanties of mud, burlap, and tin.

But housing is only one aspect of the high cost of accommodating people in heavily populated cities. Water, waste disposal, health facilities, police and fire protection, streets, transport, recreation, and schools all require much heavier outlays per capita in big cities, generally without achieving comparable standards. Per capita costs are high because the value of land is high and because of the high material and labor costs of the more complex installations needed to meet the requirements of large numbers of people.

The cost of transportation on a per capita basis becomes higher in large urban centers as the shift is made from surface streets to expressways and grade separated structures. In smaller cities the bus can provide public transit without exclusive rights of way, but for high density areas expensive rail facilities are required. High urban transport costs are also en-

[7] Catherine B. Wurster, "Urban Living Conditions, Overhead Costs, and the Development Pattern," in Turner (ed.), op. cit., p. 293.

[8] Charles Abrams, Man's Struggle for Shelter in an Urbanizing World (Massachusetts Institute of Technology Press, 1964), p. 52.

countered even when the necessary transport investments are not made, for much of the cost of moving goods is the cost of congestion: the high operating costs and time loss in overburdened terminals or on congested streets.

These difficulties are present in all cities, but their magnitude reaches much greater proportions as city size increases. City housing conditions worsen with increasing size. In Calcutta four out of ten families are squatters or sleep in the streets. The shortage of housing is estimated at 600,000 units. More than two million people with no housing are forced to double up with other families or have no shelter at all.[9] Families living in one room comprise 67 percent of the total in the four largest Indian cities compared to 44 percent for the urban average and 34 percent for rural areas. Households with less than fifty square feet of floor space per capita comprise 70 percent of the total in Calcutta and 14 percent in rural families.[10]

Congestion on the streets and transport facilities of India's major cities has reached crisis proportions. In Old Delhi the streets of the Nair Bazaar are completely clogged with bullock carts, trucks, and people. At the warehouses and booking agents no off-street space is provided for the hundreds of vehicles waiting to load or unload, and merchandise of every description covers the sidewalks. It is practically impossible to drive a vehicle through the area after mid-morning. The scene is duplicated in large cities and small—in the colossal confusion along the thoroughfare serving Bombay's Alexandria Docks, in the morning and evening rush on Calcutta's Hooghly River Bridge, and on the teeming main arteries of Kanpur, Lucknow, and Hyderabad.

The Hooghly River, which divides the twin cities of Calcutta and Howrah, has heavily influenced the street and highway system that has evolved in the metropolitan area. The geographi-

---

[9] See also Nirmal Kumar Bose, "Calcutta: A Premature Metropolis," *Scientific American*, September 1965, pp. 91–102.

[10] Wurster, *op. cit.*, p. 280.

Commuters crossing the silt-clogged Hooghly River by Howrah Bridge.
Alan Villiers © 1963 National Geographic Society

cal constriction of development along the narrow strips of high
land on the river has resulted in daily major traffic bottlenecks
on the principal highways. These, in poor repair, are lined
on both sides by crowded shops and houses; business is con-
ducted on the pavement; automobiles, trucks, pedestrians, hand-
carts, rickshas, bicycles, bullock carts, and miscellaneous animals jam the roadway.[11]

The Hooghly River is also a major barrier to road and rail
communications. At only two points can road traffic cross the
53 miles of the river between north and south. The strain on
the highway bridge linking Calcutta and Howrah is adversely
affecting the economic function of the metropolis. Especially
damaging are the difficulties of traveling to and from the port,
and between Howrah Station (with its rail links to the hinterland) on one side of the river and the central business district
of Calcutta on the other. In 1947, 12,000 motor vehicles crossed
the bridge daily; by 1964, this figure had almost tripled.

Between 1956 and 1964, the number of trucks in Calcutta
increased by 52 percent and passenger vehicles by 43 percent.
This substantial growth of motor transportation without par-
allel expansion in road construction and improvement in traffic
control has exacerbated the severe congestion. In the five-year
period 1960 to 1965, the number of accidents in Calcutta rose
20 percent.

Transit services in Calcutta and its immediate environs are
provided by buses operated by the Calcutta State Transport Corporation and by trains operated by the Calcutta Tramways
Company. Together these systems serve 802 million transit passengers annually. Both trams and buses are grossly overloaded.
Trams with a maximum seating capacity of 80 often carry as
many as 200. Passengers clinging to the outside and struggling
for a foothold on the running boards are common sights.

[11] Data from Government of West Bengal, Calcutta Metropolitan Planning
Organization, *Basic Development Plan: Calcutta Metropolitan District, 1966-
1986* (Calcutta, 1966).

The tramways have operated at maximum capacity since the mid-1940's, with little improvement. Today more than 300,000 passengers cross the Howrah Bridge by bus and tram on an average weekday, and there are numerous other travel corridors in the city where transit passenger volumes exceed 150,000 daily. By 1976 the demand for mass transportation services in Calcutta is expected to be double the 1962 figure.

The two main railway stations serving suburban commuters accommodate more than 200,000 passengers daily. Over the past ten years, the number of rail commuters has doubled. During the morning peak hours, 29 trains arrive at these two railway stations carrying 53,000 suburban commuters. This is an average loading of 1,850 per train.

The traffic situation is not much better in Bombay.[12] During the decade of the sixties, while the population of Bombay increased by half, the number of motor vehicles more than doubled. Four million passengers were moving daily by bus and rail, and mass transportation patrons were increasing at an annual rate of 4 percent. The capacity of the transport equipment available to carry this load is chronically inadequate. Antiquated vehicles, poor maintenance, and notorious overloading are typical. And as the number of people and motor vehicles mounts, so do requirements for street widening, parking facilities, traffic control, new freight yards and terminals, railway relocations, grade separations, and rapid transit.

Improving the Use of Existing Facilities

The first approach to the solution of transport and related problems associated with urbanization is to assure that urban transport facilities for both passengers and freight are made to operate as efficiently as they can, and that all additions to trans-

[12] Wilbur Smith and Associates, *Bombay Traffic and Transportation Study* (Smith & Assoc., 1963), Vol. 1.

port capacity are integrated with plans for development of the urban areas themselves. At the same time the demand for transportation must be controlled by planning the purposes and densities of land use, by controlling traffic movements, and by arrangements to minimize unnecessary movement.

The Fourth Plan attaches special importance to the effective use of investments already made. Improvement in the supply of transport services can be achieved to a considerable degree in just this way. Methods involve the efficient routing and timing of traffic, the clearing of major arteries for the movement of motor vehicles, and the routing of through traffic around built-up areas that are not points of origin or destination. Investment in streets can also be reduced by furnishing off-street terminal and parking space for motor vehicles now, before the automotive revolution gains further momentum. Otherwise Indian cities will be forced to use costly streets for vehicle storage when they are needed to move traffic. By shifting parked vehicles from street to off-street accommodations, the financial responsibility for terminals can be shifted from the public to the private sector.

Transport capacity can also be increased through a more selective use of street systems by specific types of traffic. Routes can be designated for the exclusive use of buses, at least in commuting hours, and specific streets or entire areas can be set aside for pedestrians. The importance of good accommodations for foot travel is indicated by the fact that half of all Bombay employees walk to their jobs. Only 1.4 percent travel by automobile.

An additional way to make more effective use of transport facilities is to spread the traffic more evenly over the day. The problems of the commuter are unnecessarily compounded by the fact that most employees report for work at the same time and leave together in the evening. The total costs of accommodating such peak loads, plus the unmeasured costs in wear and tear on human beings, are sufficient to warrant staggered hours of arrival and departure. There is no evidence that staggered work hours will result in loss of efficiency in the operation of most business firms. If the time and discomfort of commuting could be eased in this way, the result might well be greater worker efficiency as well as savings in transport investment.

A variety of other solutions that are essentially traffic engineering include the designation of one-way streets, the control of turning movements, the generous use of paint on street surfaces to organize traffic movements, and the establishment and enforcement of appropriate rules of the road. Although these remedies may seem superficial, in reality they are among the most effective means of assuring the efficient use of large investments already made in urban transport infrastructure.

American and European experience indicates how traffic controls can improve the efficiency of streets and highways. The elimination of curb parking, for example, may increase street capacity by 50 percent. Where streets have been converted to one-way traffic, traffic per lane and average speeds have often been doubled, and accidents cut in half. Pavement markings have proved highly effective in channeling traffic. Proper use of traffic signal lights can also improve the flow of vehicles, and the prohibition of left turns can add capacity equivalent to a full lane. The establishment of preferential streets for through traffic by the erection of stop signs is another universally effective device.

More drastic changes include removal of rail yards, terminals, and surface rail lines from congested areas, their relocation on the periphery, and the development of coordinated truck-rail freight distribution systems that minimize congestion. In the passenger field, public transit by buses on exclusive rights of way should be attempted before resort to costly subway construction. Elevated structures for either rail or highway should be avoided as both costly and a positive barrier to improvement of the urban environment. Where roadways are depressed, the air rights above them can be made available for buildings, public parks, housing, and other uses.

Broadening the Concept of Urban Transport

In contemplating the very large investments in basic urban transport facilities, it is important to conceive of transport developments as part of a total integrated system of movement. Highways, parking, terminals, bus service, rail commuter services, and the regulation of traffic movements all need to be considered as parts of an interrelated network. A transportation agency at local level could help assure the physical coordination of transport facilities, the establishment of consistent fare policies, and the pooling of revenues for all transport. The agency could also relate the problems of freight distribution to programs for improving passenger movement.

But this is not enough. Plans for transport need to be part of the total effort to build better urban communities. Urban transport investment not only provides capacity for movement but serves as the framework of the urban area. Well-planned transport facilities can help bring about satisfactory neighborhood designs, and can provide for the layout of industrial estates, commercial centers, and transport terminals. If transport is properly designed in conjunction with housing, employment areas, and community facilities, the result may be an absolute reduction in the volume of unnecessary travel. The construction of coordinated rail-truck-bus terminals can also help to reduce street congestion.

Road and street plans, as part of the urban system, can help to assure light and air and recreation space, as well as sites for future public facilities. In India's growing cities, land should be acquired now for major arterials and open space that will someday be needed. This can be done either by outright purchase before land values have risen, or by the purchase of development rights from the owners. The goal may be to use the land later for public purposes or to preserve a good supply of agricultural land close by for feeding the urban population. The preservation of open land adjacent to major intercity highways may also help to avoid the ribbon development that typically chokes the highway as the city moves outward.

Indian cities can be expected to spread out over a much wider area as dependence on foot travel and bicycles gives way to greater use of motorized transport. A forward-looking policy of land acquisition and control, in keeping with comprehensive urban and transport planning, may be the most important step to bring about a more rational pattern of growth in existing cities.

Green belts around the city can be one means of setting geographic limits to urban sprawl. The importance of belt highways and bypass routes around the city as a means of keeping long-distance traffic out of the downtown areas has already been demonstrated in India, Japan, and elsewhere. These routes, along with additional reservation of land for agriculture, can help reduce future congestion and the large outlays required to cope with it.

Land acquisition for transport and other public purposes can also have a significant role in financial solutions. Land acquired for planned transport and other purposes means both lower acquisition costs and the opportunity to combine transport building with provision of housing and other community facilities. Excess land acquired in connection with roadway construction permits later sale or lease by the city and the recoupment for the public of the increase in values resulting from the transport investment.

The task of finding satisfactory transport remedies, then, lies not only in supplying additional capacity but in using transport to influence the environment and to control the factors governing transport demand. Studies of urban development through computer simulation may ultimately make these complex relationships more understandable and measurable, and thus provide better techniques for land use and transport planning.[13] We know that different types of land use generate different volumes

[13] At Michigan State University, a Ford Foundation project in community development problems is making use of computer simulation to aid decision-makers in measuring the short- and long-run effects of responses to the need for housing, recreation, transport, and other capital improvement programs.

of traffic per acre. Commercial uses are generally the highest generators, and public recreation use is the lowest. Home-to-work trips account for the greatest concentration of traffic and establish peak transport requirements. Various types of industry create heavy accumulations of freight. The responsibility of urban planners is to seek arrangements and densities for these land uses that avoid unmanageable concentrations of people and economic activity.

Restricting Big City Growth

Besides dealing directly with existing congestion, it may be possible to slow down the growth of the largest cities where the solution to transport and other problems is so difficult and costly. This might be accomplished by offering incentives to encourage growth in smaller places and by banning certain types of industrial development in the urban agglomerations that have already become unmanageable. With the growing efficiency of transport and communications technology, it should be possible for moderate-sized cities to absorb a larger share of urban growth and to operate with relatively greater economy and effectiveness. The densities in the already overcrowded metropolises have reached the point where gross inefficiencies are unavoidable.

Already population densities in Metropolitan Calcutta are among the highest in the world. The number of people living within the physical boundaries of the District has almost tripled in the last forty years. Calcutta's average densities are 159 persons per developed acre and 294 persons per residential acre. They are the highest Indian population densities by a considerable margin. (See Table IV–4.) In many Indian rural villages, residential densities are as low as five to ten persons per acre.

Under present circumstances the individual city is helpless to reverse the present trends in urban settlement that determine the magnitude of its problems. As industrial growth and the

TABLE IV–4.   *Developed and Residential Area Densities in Selected Major Cities*
(Persons per acre)

City	Developed land density	Residential land density
Calcutta	159.4	293.6
Delhi	64.5	196.0
Bangalore	76.9	142.9
Ahmedabad	88.5	227.3
New York	43.6	163.9
Los Angeles	12.3	23.3

Source: Calcutta Metropolitan Planning Organization, *Basic Development Plan: Calcutta Metropolitan District, 1966–1986* (Calcutta: CMPO, 1966), p. 16.

shift from farm to factory continue, these trends, added to natural population growth, promise to magnify the economic liabilities of large urban concentrations. The possibility that industrialization will continue to focus on Calcutta, Bombay, Kanpur, and a limited number of metropolitan centers compels attention to feasible alternatives. If the present trend is allowed to continue, the result will be not only intractable cities, but an ever wider gap between a few urban-industrial enclaves and the vast hinterland of rural India. Both the city and the country will be victims of the failure to introduce more desirable spatial concepts into urban planning.

A possible escape from the excessive build-up of a few supercities lies in channeling urban growth into small or moderate-sized communities where planned expansion could attract population and create more viable cities. An important lesson can be learned from the experience of countries that have preceded India into the urban-industrial era. England, France, the United States, and other populous countries are now discovering the high costs of planless urban development and uncontrolled urban sprawl. Deterioration of transportation, housing, and public services and the lack of recreation facilities and other amenities are compelling extensive slum clearance and urban redevelopment, as well as the construction of entirely new cities. The cost of correcting past mistakes is staggering. Vast areas of urban decay will have to be reclaimed and new patterns

of urban life will need to be designed to provide a more satisfactory urban environment.

It is now possible to plan a more dispersed pattern of urbanization because of recent technological breakthroughs, especially
advances in transport. Transport technology is now an agent
of dispersal rather than of concentration and congestion. Many
sites at a locational disadvantage in an age dominated by rail
and water movement can flourish on the much larger network
of highways, with the added support of travel by air. With
further advances in aircraft performance, this latest addition
to the transport network will provide more economical connections and access to every part of the country. Other innovations
that may be equally important in advancing new patterns of
urban development include low-cost telephone services made
possible by new methods of ground and satellite transmission;
innovations in producing and delivering electric power; the use
of radio and television; and agricultural processing industries
which can locate close to sources of supply.

An examination of some of the economic trade-offs between
transport and other public services necessary for urban life
indicates that a policy of decentralizing some of the major employment centers can offer notable savings. To build new decen-
tralized workplaces every few years, at the edge of the already
built-up area, is likely to result in a considerably lower total
cost than a policy of adding new workplaces around the central
area. This is especially true in cities where growth of some
magnitude is expected to take place.[14]

In a centralized city pattern, there may be a ring of vacant
land left between the initially built-up central workplace and
the residential area to provide for future expansion. This results in lengthening the trip to work, and as industry expands
to fill the vacant space there is inevitable destruction of housing
and commercial facilities that are still in good condition. A de-

---

[14] Robert Jones, "Transport and Urban Design: Some Trade-offs Related to
Housing," in Edwin T. Haefele (ed.), *Relating Transport to National Policy*
(Brookings Institution, 1968).

centralized pattern, in contrast, can provide housing closer to a central administrative and business district, shortening commuter trips and reducing transport cost for those who work at the center. Manufacturing, on the other hand, can be dispersed on the periphery, again close to housing.

Whatever the urban design solutions, India has the opportunity to plan consciously for its most rapid period of urban growth, and thereby to achieve both a better urban environment and a reduction in the required investment. The task will be to establish a national plan for urbanization to guide the nation's urban development, avoiding the waste of supporting villages that are too small and metropolitan areas that are too large. "Once the alternatives are understood, the idea of steering much of India's mass of industrial location decisions during the sixties toward some middle ground . . . has a compelling appeal."[15]

A first step toward guiding India's urban growth is the designation of favorable sites for accommodating future population expansion, including both existing moderate-sized communities and possibly new sites as well. To make a start, existing cities should be selected that could absorb more people and industry if satisfactory accommodations were supplied. There are some 141 municipalities in India with populations of between 50,000 and 100,000. These medium-sized cities are the most likely candidates for further industrial development. Many of the 515 additional cities in the 20,000 to 50,000 population class could also be expanded to advantage, as well as 800 other communities with populations of 10,000 to 20,000. Focusing on these cities provides the most immediate solution to overcongestion.

It will be necessary to assess the special attributes and characteristics of these cities to determine whether or in what ways they should be encouraged to grow. Some may be well situated for certain types of industry, already well supplied with transportation, or capable of being made more accessible. Be-

[15] John P. Lewis, *Quiet Crisis in India* (Brookings Institution, 1962), p. 179.

cause of raw material supplies and other resources, some may be potential centers for manufacturing, and others for educational and research activities. Elsewhere the promise may lie in agro-industries or in cities that could serve as new ocean ports.

Methods of enlarging such cities are indicated by the wide range of incentives being offered by the State of Maharashtra to encourage new industrial enterprises to locate away from Bombay in smaller urban communities. They include the financing and conduct of feasibility studies for new industrial establishments, reduced charges for water and electricity, tax abatement, freedom from octroi taxes on building materials, subsidized housing, and preference for relocated industries in government purchasing.

But the rapid growth in urban population and the lack of suitable existing cities may make it necessary, in addition, to establish entirely new towns where modern transport and other technology make it economically possible and desirable to do so. These might be satellite communities near existing big cities or independent settlements away from any large city, selected on the basis of climate, geography, and resource endowment.

Building New Cities

The new city idea is not new to Indians. The contrast between a planned New Delhi and a relatively planless Old Delhi provides an example of what is physically possible. Despite high costs, the breathing space and orderly setting that Le Corbusier provided in Chandigarh, the new capital of the Punjab, give a hint of what could be done for industrial and commercial cities. A planned community of very much earlier origins is Jaipur, in the State of Rajasthan, and there are other more contemporary new towns in India built as a unit by the government or by industrial corporations. All of them offer certain advantages such as cheap land, maximum freedom to accommodate future expansion, and minimum problems of local transportation.

It is often mistakenly thought that India is so overcrowded that practically no vacant land remains for new settlement. Actually, for the country as a whole, population density averages 368 persons per square mile. Japan has 673 persons per square mile. England has 874. The population density of New Jersey is 642. Making room, as the Belgians and the Dutch seem to have done, means learning how to make the best use of the land there is.

The building of new cities requires such conditions as relatively flat land, a supply of fresh water, and access to raw materials. On the basis of these three minimal factors, it has been concluded that 10 percent of the total Indian continent qualifies for urban settlement. Bengal and Orissa seemed to be most favorably suited for urbanization, while Madras might be the focus of an urban region that could support as many as 60 to 80 million persons.[16]

The justification of using scarce capital to build new cities rather than permit incremental growth of present overcrowded urban concentrations is difficult to establish in the short run. For in big cities the infrastructure is already there, and the scarcity of investment capital suggests making more and more use of what is already in place, hoping that the day of reckoning will be postponed. But ultimately a city becomes so unwieldy that it makes economic sense to avoid the costly consequences by diverting growth into new centers where the necessary infrastructure has to be started from scratch.

The question to be answered is at what point the addition of a given number of people to an existing large city can be expected to cost more than the urban advantages realized, and whether the benefit-cost relationship would be more favorable if these people were to be accommodated in existing smaller communities, where expansion would be advantageous for both

[16] Richard Meier, "Relations of Technology to the Design of Very Large Cities," in Turner (ed.), op. cit., pp. 302–3.

the existing community as a whole and those included in the incremental growth.

Initially the cost of creating an entirely new community is high. New investments in basic facilities require heavy capital outlays, and since a certain minimum investment is required before the new settlement can function, per capita costs will be high until the population build-up is completed. In an already existing city, on the other hand, most of the added costs of accommodating more people will be incurred as gradual increments to existing public services, or as rising prices for housing and other private goods. Part of the burden will be absorbed by avoiding the necessary public expenditures and accepting lower standards of service instead. The resulting increase in social costs may take the form of a high incidence of disease, poor education, unemployment, transport congestion, or lower efficiency in all types of economic activities.

The hope of avoiding the high costs of urban agglomerations through building up intermediate towns rests on the assumption that geographic concentration is often no longer necessary for realizing the economies of large-scale operations. Close-knit relations among cities may be achieved by the lower cost and higher speed of intercity transport and communications. Entrepreneurs can now use the telephone and the airplane to oversee activities that may be widely separated. In many industries new methods of production and marketing made possible by motor trucking may make dispersal more desirable than concentration. It may soon be as cheap or quick to conduct intercity communications as it is to get from one end to the other of a city that is overgrown and highly congested.

Thus the task for Indian planning is to help create a more desirable economic geography suited to carrying out the industrial development program. The Planning Commission and regional planning authorities will need to explore the costs and advantages of alternative urban designs, and to provide instruments and incentives for directing the course of urban growth in ways that avoid unnecessary costs and undesirable living conditions. Otherwise the growing diseconomies of excessive concentration can easily cancel the anticipated gains from future economic growth.

Creating Market Towns

Along with new cities and the expansion of small cities to disperse urban population, an additional need mentioned in the previous chapter is for market towns to aid in the commercialization of agriculture. More market towns are necessary to provide farmers with a convenient place to bring their produce, and to supply warehouses, processing plants, consumer goods, and credit facilities. It has been noted that in many parts of India these and other services have been made available through the establishment of regulated markets. The 1,000 regulated market towns now operating are located predominantly in cities of 10,000 to 50,000 population. Their distribution throughout the country is uneven, with one state accounting for one-third of the total. If full coverage were to be provided in all states, there would have to be nearly 5,000 more of these agro-centers throughout the country.[17]

These requirements afford an opportunity to concentrate infrastructure investments to serve the demands of agriculture and at the same time to help disperse urban-industrial growth in more moderate-sized cities. The infrastructure investments are going to be made in any event. A selected number of communities can thus be provided with the necessary public services to accelerate their growth and permit them to serve as new centers for industry, markets for agriculture, and distribution centers for farm supplies and consumer goods. Principal infrastructure requirements will be schools and hospitals, storage facilities, fertilizer depots, high-voltage power lines, water filtration plants, sewer and sanitation facilities, agricultural

[17] National Council of Applied Economic Research, *Market Towns and Spatial Development in India* (New Delhi: NCAER, 1965), p. 68.

processing plants, supply depots, and improved transport and communications. Transport connections to permit these centers to function will be of key importance: road construction, airports and air services, bus routes, trucking lines, and access to the rail system.

One of the hoped-for results of building such growth points is that they may attract part of the rural population that would otherwise move to the larger cities. Additional numbers might remain in agriculture because of the added economic incentives that market towns create. Still other villagers, though dissatisfied with farming, may find it attractive to continue living in their villages, but to bicycle or bus to work in the nearby agro-industrial centers. These factors could help slow the migration to the metropolis, and lead to new vitality in smaller urban settlements. They might also help to reduce the frustrations of living at subsistence level in cities that have grown beyond their economic limits.

However it is done, the trends toward urban overconcentration on the one hand and excessive dispersal of rural villages on the other need to be reversed. The national urban plan must comprise both large cities and small and be geared to meeting the future needs of agriculture, industry, and the expanding population. It will be necessary to program and time-phase the development of the transport and communications systems to serve this planned network of urban settlements, and to concentrate the allocation of public investment in the places scheduled to become the key cities and towns of the future. These outlays, together with government tax incentives and other inducements, can encourage and support a new and more viable economic geography for India.

CHAPTER V

Transporting Ideas and Information

Tнᴇ ᴅɪꜰꜰᴇʀᴇɴᴄᴇꜱ ɪɴ ᴋɪɴᴅ and in magnitude between the transport problems of rural and urban India are a reminder of the widening gap that separates the village from the city. The dimensions of the gap are the inevitable product of the inability to move information.

In India today, as in the rest of the low-income areas of the world, the inadequate and often impassable rural roads are almost the sole means of disseminating news, spreading ideas, and maintaining social and political ties. These are the principal channels that make it possible for rural people to share at all in the innovations stemming from the scientific revolution. The high volume of passenger travel by road and rail relative to the movement of freight reflects the fact that in a nation with a high rate of illiteracy people have to move to communicate. But most people have neither the time nor money to travel. So their lives and thoughts range no more than a short distance from where they were born, with only an occasional trip for a fortunate few between home and the nearest town.

The Role of Telecommunications

Historically it was like this for everybody. Transport and communications were the same, because communication was possible only through the transportation of a message. This is why the Post Office in the United States has always had a keen interest in transport, from the early development of roads for rural mail routes to the payment of subsidies to airlines. With the development of telegraph and telephone services, however, the link between transportation and communications was broken, and the gap has since been widened by radio and television. Communications were extremely limited when they depended entirely on transport, but now, through electromagnetic means, they provide instant and global coverage. The slowness, high cost, and limited capacity of the transport system can now be supplemented by new methods of transmission with prodigious capacity for overcoming space and time.

India has hardly passed the threshold of this new world of instant communications. When there is urgent business to be done, it may be more efficient to travel hundreds of miles by airplane to discuss matters in person than to depend on telephone connections. To those who live in the villages, the information that farmers need to know about markets, weather, prices, and new techniques rarely penetrates at all. When it does, the reporting by travelers and merchants is sporadic, unreliable, and unselective. Even agricultural extension workers who visit farmers to advise and demonstrate are unable to cover enough territory or make sufficiently frequent appearances. To do so is not practical when the supply of instructors is limited and the rate of travel slow.

In the state of Uttar Pradesh, for example, there are 112,000 rural villages to be contacted, containing over a million farm families. Each village-level worker has to help 600 to 1,000 families spread over 10 to 12 villages. The large number of people who need help, and the fact that 80 percent of them are illiterate, make the communication of agricultural information costly and time-consuming. "Within the time and resources available, it is not possible for village level workers, or Block Development officers or the District Development officers to approach each family, even once a year." [1]

[1] Government of Uttar Pradesh, *Draft Fourth Five-Year Plan of Agriculture and Allied Sectors, 1966–71* (Lucknow, 1967), Vol. I, p. 216.

In the twentieth century, even a good transport system is a
poor substitute for a system of communications, but where
transport is poor it is even less satisfactory. In these circumstances
knowledge of the outside world is minimal for the rural population, and the very concept of economic progress is foreign to those
who live beyond the sound barrier. This is a critical defect in
India's efforts to feed her people, for "the crux of the Indian agricultural problem is to induce a breakthrough in the traditional
attitudes of the farmer, so that on his own volition he takes to
better farming practices."[2]

There is no question that in recent years more information has
been getting through to the Indian villages and has contributed to
agricultural achievements. During the first three five-year plans,
India increased foodgrain production 50 percent. While the
drought of 1965–66 temporarily masked these gains, the record
is a remarkable one because it was achieved with limited fertilizer and primitive tools. Indian farmers have been respond-
ing to "new aspirations spreading through the countryside by
informal communication. . . ."[3] It is not unlikely that this re-
sponse has been made possible by the thousands of miles of
rudimentary roads built in the countryside during the past fifteen
years, even though they are passable only part of the year, and
perhaps only for foot travellers or bullock carts. Credit must
also be given to radio, for transistors have become the prized
possession of a limited number of village leaders and school
teachers who share the listening with friends.

The importance of communicating basic knowledge to rural
people who lack formal education is suggested by an analysis of
the factors that have contributed to the growth of the American
economy. An estimate for the period 1929 to 1957 attributes
one-fourth of the growth of national product to the improved

[2] Ashok Mitra, "Tax Burden for Indian Agriculture," in Ralph Braibanti and
Joseph J. Spengler (eds.), Administration and Economic Development in India
(Duke University Press, 1963), p. 297.
[3] Charles E. Lindblom, "Has India an Economic Future?" Foreign Affairs,
January 1966, p. 242.

quality of the labor force brought about by education. In addition, advances in knowledge relevant to production permitted greater output per unit of input and may have contributed another 20 percent to total growth.[4] While the measurements are arguable, they focus attention on the reality that education, research, and communications have a highly important combined role in improving economic performance.

In India considerable progress has been made in rural education for those of school age, but little has been done to upgrade the knowledge of those already engaged in farm activities who are often doubly isolated from the educational process—by distance and by illiteracy. Yet unless the rural population in this category can become better informed, it can scarcely be expected to participate in the tasks required for accelerated economic development. The potentials of today's technology offer a major new hope through trade-offs between the movement of people and the movement of information. India has the opportunity to make a more effective allocation of its resources between transport and the new media of communications.

The Expansion of Radio

The inadequacy of India's telecommunications is measured by comparisons with other low-income countries. The number of telephones per 10,000 inhabitants is 16 in India, 104 in the United Arab Republic, 235 in Colombia, 506 in Greece. The number of radios per 10,000 people is 91 in India, 754 in the United Arab Republic, 978 in Greece, and 1,716 in Colombia. (See Table V–1.) Thus the use of radios has far outstripped the telephone.

In the First Plan, the allocation to radio broadcasting was about one-tenth of one percent of the total resources made available. In

[4] Edward F. Denison, "The Sources of Economic Growth in the United States and the Alternatives before Us" (Supplementary Paper No. 13, Committee for Economic Development, 1962), pp. 267–68.

TABLE V–1.   *Number of Telephones and Radios in Selected Countries, 1964*

Country	Number of telephones		Number of radios	
	Total (in thousands)	Per 10,000 inhabitants	Total (in thousands)	Per 10,000 inhabitants
Algeria	140	128	1,500[a]	1,367
Ethiopia	21	9	150[b]	68
Ghana	33	44	555	736
Morocco	142	110	650	502
Nigeria	60[c]	11	600	106
United Arab Republic	301	104	2,178	754
Mexico	725	183	7,281	1,837
Argentina	1,472	668	6,200	2,815
Chile	250	294	1,500[b]	1,766
Colombia	410	235	3,000[b]	1,716
Peru	132	117	2,000[a]	1,770
India	763	16	4,315	91
Iran	180	79	1,600[a]	700
Japan	9,712	1,002	19,666	2,029
Pakistan	121	12	549	54
Philippines	152	49	1,225	392
Turkey	334	109	2,177	710
Czechoslovakia	1,399	995	3,696	2,629
Greece	431	506	832	978
Spain	2,509	801	4,000	1,276

Source: United Nations, *Statistical Yearbook, 1965* (New York, 1966).
a. 1963.
b. 1962.
c. Includes the former British Cameroons.

the Second Plan, it was two-tenths of one percent, and in the Third Plan it was reduced to one-eighth of one percent.[5]

India's 31 radio stations now cover 62 percent of the nation's area, where 77 percent of the population live. But the percentage of people actually affected is small. In 1966 there were some 5 million individual transistor receiving sets for the nation's nearly 500 million people, most of them in urban areas.

[5] Government of India, Ministry of Information and Broadcasting, "Report of the Committee on Broadcasting and Information Media on Television for India" (mimeographed, 1965), p. 3.

All India Radio has installed community listening sets in about 150,000 villages. Some 7,500 to 8,000 rural radio forums have been organized, but spot-checking in the field has revealed that many are inactive.

Many difficulties afflict the typical community listening arrangements. One is that at any given time approximately half the sets are out of order, awaiting the repairs that are always needed more frequently when a set is used by a large number of people. Listening is also impeded by a reluctance among villagers of various castes to join in community listening sessions. Many of the rural forums are not attended by women, artisans, landless laborers and others who would find instruction especially useful.

The main approaches to more effective use of radio lie first in providing larger numbers of low-cost individual transistors so that more villagers can own them; second, in improving programs of local interest to rural residents; and third, in making better use of radio for the classroom.

According to UNESCO, a rural community should have a minimum of five radio sets per one hundred people. To meet even this minimum standard, India should have 25 million radios, or five times as many as are now available. But the UNESCO standards are much too low, and the need in a country as large as India is far greater. If India were to have the same ratio of radios to people as Japan, twenty times as many sets would be needed, or a total of 100 million rather than the present 5 million. The importance of approaching such a level as soon as possible suggests a mass production program to multiply the availability of low-cost transistorized receivers.

In 1963 India produced about 45,000 low-cost transistor radios, 30,000 of them community receivers. The actual number of radios available at the end of the Third Plan fell far short of the target, and the Fourth Plan target of 400,000 receivers seems unlikely to be achieved with the limited resources available and at projected costs.

All India Radio estimates that a receiving set could be produced at a factory cost of 40 rupees with components imported
free of duty, and for 65 rupees if duty is levied. The cost would
be 75 rupees if Indian-produced components were used. Import
duties for components such as tubes, loud speakers, and raw
materials amount to 70 percent of the cost of a low-priced radio.
Yet imported components cost less after the duty than home-
produced components, which are manufactured at high cost because of small-scale output and labor-intensive methods. Making
allowance for distribution costs, excise duty, sales tax, and profits,
a radio made with indigenous components could sell at a retail
price of 110 rupees. If the government bought 2 million transistorized receivers from abroad, and the import duty were waived,
such radios could be marketed at a retail price of under 40
rupees. But in the longer run, domestic output on a large scale
could be expected to furnish sets at much lower cost than is
now possible.

In addition to personal transistor sets, Fourth Plan objectives
include the manufacture of 500,000 transistorized community
radio receivers costing 400 rupees each. Total cost would be 20
crores, or nearly $27 million. Other radio costs estimated by the
Committee on Broadcasting and Information Media include
service and maintenance centers to repair receiving sets, and a
large number of low-powered transmitters to serve rural districts. At least 30 of these transmitters are scheduled to be built
by the end of the Fourth Plan.

Radio sets alone will not be enough, however, for the programming itself has come under severe criticism. A survey of All
India Radio operations shows that only 5 to 8 percent of the
time and about the same percentage of money for radio broadcasting have been allocated to rural audiences. Programs for
rural areas are broadcast for only an hour daily. These programs
have low priority, inadequate financing, and are described as
generally unimaginative in content. The Committee studying the
matter for the Government of India has pointed out that national programs are not related to the particular needs of local

areas, that programs for farmers are at the wrong time, and that to be useful they should be repeated at convenient hours.[6]

The news broadcasts are criticized as dull and stereotyped, with too little frank discussion of both sides of public issues. It is revealing that at the Kanpur television station of the Indian Institute of Technology (I.I.T.), students base news programs on foreign radio broadcasts which they edit for later transmission in order to furnish a more meaningful account of public affairs than is available from official government sources at home. The enthusiasm of the Indian radio audience for programs from Radio Ceylon suggests that there is substantial room for improving both the information and entertainment content of domestic programs. Both have a role to play in bringing the Indian people into closer communication with the outside world and with each other.

The Beginnings of Television

As the revolution in communications continues, attention is shifting to television. In early 1967 the only television transmission in India was from the 5 kilowatt Delhi station of All-India Radio, serving a radius of 30 kilometers. Some 5,000 receivers were in operation, including over 4,000 sets in private houses, 300 community viewing sets, and 500 sets in Delhi schools.

Delhi television began in 1959 with the "Tele-Clubs," which now meet at approximately 300 schools and centers run by the Delhi Municipal Corporation. The purpose of the programs was to provide easily assimilated information and to encourage community progress. The range of subjects has included cooperatives, family planning, repair of domestic appliances, first aid, health and hygiene, kitchen gardening, disposal of waste materials, observance of traffic regulations, and opportunities for

[6] Government of India, Ministry of Information and Broadcasting, "Report of the Committee on Broadcasting and Information Media on Broadcasts for Rural Areas" (mimeographed, 1965).

careers. Feedback from viewers is provided by monthly club meetings and reports to program planners on audience reactions. The clubs have an active membership of 5,000 persons and some 25,000 viewers. (See Table V–2.)

TABLE V–2.   *Estimated Delhi Television Audience*

Type of audience	Number of televiewers
1. Schools	
Science (higher secondary classes)	36,000
English (middle)	96,000
General science (middle)	96,000
2. Tele-Clubs (community	
viewing sets)	25,000
3. Home receivers (4,000)	35,000
Total	288,000

Source: Data supplied by the Government of India, Ministry of Information and Broadcasting, New Delhi, India, 1966.

Classroom television was initiated on an experimental basis in 1961. Regular courses have been given in physics, chemistry, English, and general science. Manuals are supplied to teachers to furnish a preview of the telecast and to help prepare the students, as well as to provide follow-through instruction after the program is over. There are also TV programs aimed at instructing teachers.

In addition to classroom TV during the day, two hours of general-interest programs are transmitted in the evening. A typical program in February 1967 included a Hindi play, a documentary on Southern India's efforts to harness its water resources for power and irrigation, a surgical operation, and the news. The picture was of excellent quality; so were the program content and performance. Young people, gathered around private sets in Delhi homes, display a rapt attention that makes clear the absorbing characteristics of this new communications medium. Many children as well as grown-ups witness for the first time what the Indian people are actually accomplishing in the campaign to build a better society.

Early in 1967, Delhi TV was being extended to 81 villages in the area, with the purpose of introducing programs aimed at the needs of rural residents. Reactions to these programs will provide a basis for designing appropriate materials for village reception. The intention is also to operate mobile vans for telecasting from the villages to Delhi, thus providing urban viewers with what may be their only knowledge of rural life and its problems.

A further effort to learn more about the educational potentials of television is being made at the Television Center of the Indian Institute of Technology (I.I.T.) at Kanpur. There in early 1967 programs of general interest for student viewing included films, illustrated lectures, and round-table discussions. Since the Government of India has a monopoly on radio and television, the I.I.T. television station has been restricted to a closed circuit and may not transmit its programs even within the campus itself. Yet with little added outlay, it would be possible for the Institute to make available science courses and laboratory instruction for Kanpur school and college classrooms, as well as to conduct controlled experiments in TV programming through telecasts to nearby villages. Scientific evaluation of the impact of such programs could supply All India Radio with valuable additional information on effective methods of educational TV. A further result would be to train personnel for Indian television in future years. Student volunteers now conduct the closed-circuit system, programming approximately 14 hours a week on a budget of $27 per month.

A master plan for the extension of telecasting to other parts of India was presented in a report prepared by the Ministry of Information and Broadcasting in 1965. It called for an investment of $140 million to be expended over a 25-year period beginning in the Fourth Plan. During the Fourth Plan $5 million would be spent in establishing centers in four metropolitan areas —Madras, Bombay, Calcutta, and Kanpur. But the report criticizes the restriction of TV to urban areas and notes the large benefits that could accrue from its use in rural areas. If television were to be introduced in all 113 cities of 100,000 population and over, a range of 15 to 20 kilometers per transmitter would permit 47 percent of the total area of India to be covered, including about 250,000 villages.[7]

The cost of building the necessary telecast centers and transmitters depends on a variety of factors, including the radiating power, number of studios, and program production potentials. Original cost estimates for TV stations in the four major cities outside Delhi were approximately $1 million each, with Delhi costs of $2 million. Half the total would be foreign exchange. (See Table V–3.) Later estimates have been very much higher as the

TABLE V–3. *Initial Cost Estimates of Television Stations
in the Fourth Plan*
(In millions of rupees)

Location of station	Capital expenditures		Recurring expenditures	
	Total	Foreign exchange	Total	Foreign exchange
Bombay	8.0	3.8	3.0	0.3
Madras	8.0	3.8	3.0	0.3
Calcutta	8.0	3.8	3.0	0.3
Kanpur	8.0	3.8	3.0	0.3
Delhi	15.0	6.0	3.6	0.3
Total	47.0	21.2	15.6	1.5

Source: Data supplied by the Government of India, Ministry of Information and Broadcasting, New Delhi, India, 1966.

size and operating capabilities of the proposed stations were expanded, and daily program duration was extended from three hours to eight. In early 1967 the Ministry of Information and Broadcasting had upgraded plans for the four key centers (excluding Kanpur) to four-studio facilities with 100 kilowatt transmitters, capital investment of about $5 million each, and a foreign exchange component equal to 40 percent of the total. Recurring foreign exchange requirements for tubes, video tapes, and other

[7] Government of India, Ministry of Information and Broadcasting, "Report of the Committee on Broadcasting and Information Media on Television for India" (mimeographed, 1965).

consumable items were estimated at $800,000 per year for all four centers, exclusive of foreign film purchase.

The range in TV costs and capabilities can be understood by looking at the costs of various types of educational TV stations proposed for the United States at about the same time.[8] (See Appendix Table 17.) The projected United States network of 380 stations would include sixty stations serving large metropolitan areas and transmitting over a state-wide system. Among these would be twenty "key" stations producing color programs for national distribution. For these major centers, station costs are expected to be about $6.2 million, with average annual operating costs of $3 million. The other forty "regular" stations would be less costly. These stations would also serve major metropolitan areas, and typically consist of two large black-and-white studios, a small mobile unit, and a film production team. Capital cost would be about $3.3 million, with annual operating costs of $1.2 million.

Another class of educational TV centers suggested for the United States are so-called "standard" stations for metropolitan cities of less than 1,000,000 but over 300,000 population. These would have one well-equipped studio, a small mobile unit, and a small film unit. Capital costs were estimated at $1.7 million, with annual operating costs of $490,000. The cost of a smaller "basic" station for cities of less than 300,000 persons was estimated to be $290,000 per year, including amortization of an initial investment of $1.3 million. Repeater stations would operate on an annual budget of $85,000 per year.[9] Thus the U.S. figures indicate the considerable range of costs that might be considered in establishing India's initial television centers.

Although Indian TV plans recognize the advantages of using a communication satellite, its application in India was thought to be limited, at least in the first phase of the development plan, owing to inadequate channel capacity. It was concluded that

[8] *Public Television: A Program for Action,* The Report of the Carnegie Commission on Educational Television (Bantam Books, 1967), p. 137.
[9] *Ibid.,* pp. 139–45.

the goal of reaching India's inhabitants would be defeated if the satellite were not able to carry regional programs in different languages. Another disadvantage inherent in the state of the art was the need for installation of highly sophisticated and costly ground equipment. For the moment, the proposed plan would provide sixteen studio centers along with auxiliary centers and microwave linkages. If, at the end of this period, technological developments justify the use of a satellite, India would switch over, using repeater stations for extensive coverage of rural areas.

If the Indian TV network could be linked by a satellite repeater system, the cost would presumably be far less than that of a landline system. Earth satellites have made communication costs virtually independent of distance. For example, a synchronous satellite above India, rotating at the same speed as the earth, would provide economical transmission of voice and picture from ground station to repeater and back in three-tenths of a second despite the 44,000-mile round trip.

It may be wise for India to wait for an efficient satellite before committing large sums to expensive ground equipment. United States plans depended initially on 38,000 miles of coaxial cable and microwave relays for its educational TV network rather than a satellite, awaiting the time when the satellite would be able to transmit more power. Capital costs for this landline system were estimated at $42 million, with operating costs of $4 million per year. A satellite system would permit these costs to be avoided; ground-receiving stations would involve no more than $35,000 each, and transmitting stations about $150,000.[10]

Developing television for India, like radio, involves not just programming and transmission costs but importing and producing sets and components. Sets presently in use in India have 23-inch screens, are imported from Yugoslavia and Hungary, and cost the equivalent of about $300. India has licensed two firms to begin domestic production in about two years, when receivers with a 17-inch screen are expected to cost about $250.

[10] *Ibid.*, pp. 148, 194.

If each of India's 113 major cities were to have as many as 10,000 receivers, and if one community set were supplied to each of the 250,000 villages included in a 47 percent coverage of the nation's area, the cost of receivers would be one-third of a billion dollars. If a satellite repeater system were available to bring TV to all of India, the magnitude of the bill for receivers would be correspondingly higher.

Expanded radio and television coverage over the next ten years would involve substantial outlays and a high foreign exchange content. Is the revolution in communications important enough to warrant the expenditure, or would outlays of this magnitude be used to better advantage for improvements to the transport system?

The opportunities offered by telecommunications can be seen by comparing television with road transport as a means of transmitting information. The construction of 50,000 miles of local roads at an average cost of $4,000 per mile would permit the movement of information (and goods) to tens of thousands of isolated Indian villages for a total cost of $200 million for the roadways. The work might take five years, and motor vehicles to make effective use of the system would increase the cost. Messages would get moved, but slowly.

An alternative to this system might be the construction of 113 TV stations covering half the country with an aerial network reaching 250,000 villages, over which information would be able to move at the speed of light. The cost, including 250,000 TV receivers plus ground communications, would be about the same as the road system minus vehicles. School and adult education programs could be expected to reach at least 100 televiewers per village, or a daily total of 25 million.[11]

To what extent should television be employed as an initial substitute for roads to make an immediate attack on isolation? To judge the possibilities, at this stage of the communications revolu-

[11] Estimated costs include an average of $500,000 per TV station, $300 per community TV set, and the costs of the necessary coaxial cable and microwave relays.

tion, reliance has to be placed on examples of TV experience in a variety of circumstances.

Effects of Television Instruction

Thus far the effects on Indian students as a result of formal teaching by TV are impressive but not dramatic. In Delhi, students are learning more or better with television than without it, and television participants receive slightly better examination grades than those not attending television schools. The teaching process is also undergoing a change for the better. But, "in spite of the achievement much remains to be done before the potentialities of television as an aid to teaching are fully recognized and before they are fully realized even within the existing framework."[12]

In Samoa several years ago fewer than half the school-age children were attending classes, instructors were untrained, and few teaching materials were available. It was concluded that educational television would be the fastest way to bring the educational system to reasonable standards. A transmitter was erected on the summit of a 1,600-foot mountain, 26 new consolidated schools were built to replace the isolated village schools, and three TV channels were used to beam 90 lessons a week to primary grades. In 1965 three more channels were in use for high school classes. Student interest has continued high, teachers have responded well to the demanding requirements of the new medium, and as a side effect parents have gained something of a liberal education through this first introduction to the modern world.[13]

The effect on adults is especially significant, and overemphasis on the classroom as the appropriate audience for educational TV misses this point. India's education needs are universal, and are

[12] "Neurath Report" (New Delhi: Ford Foundation, 1966).
[13] Martha L. Fiedler, "ETV Goes Way Out," *American Education*, March 1967, p. 15.

just as important for those outside the formal educational system as for children attending school. For millions without formal education, television offers the chance to make up for schooling opportunities never realized. The speed of TV and its capacity for compressing up-to-date information offers unparalleled opportunities for transporting knowledge. The role of television is to deliver new understanding to all of India.

This broader role of TV instruction has been demonstrated in Japan, where UNESCO's 64 tele-clubs inaugurated in the late fifties had a pervasive effect on the participants. A series of programs on agricultural techniques introduced the early planting of rice where this had not been tried before. Many farmers for the first time began spraying to reduce insect damage to trees; others made the unusual decision to purchase equipment jointly to improve irrigation. Some villages with only foot paths began a movement to have a network of agricultural roads constructed. After villagers heard a program on the reallocation of land, 70 percent of the farmers discussed the subject at a series of follow-up meetings and agreed to carry out needed reforms. In many test villages tele-club members were persuaded to undertake a plan for collective use of farm machinery.[14] It is not improbable that the communications provided by 5 million television sets and 20 million radios in Japan have contributed in many other ways to the performance of Japanese agriculture and industry. Certainly the major impact of television in the West has not been through its classroom use, but through the broadening of horizons experienced by all televiewers, the result of instant communication of visual information.

The Effectiveness of Radio

In all parts of the world the radio is also proving its effectiveness in adult education and in the schools. To test the responsiveness of radio listeners to basic health broadcasts, for

[14] UNESCO, *Rural Television in Japan* (1960), pp. 146, 155.

example, receivers were temporarily installed in 180 locations in South Korea, and sample checks made before and after the programs to measure the impact. After hearing the program once, almost all listeners had learned how encephalitis is transmitted; knowledge of the source of typhoid fever rose fifty percent, and belief that tuberculosis is inherited dropped by more than half.[15]

It has been shown that with classroom radios as teaching aids children can be taught to read and write and that the effectiveness of scarce teaching personnel can be multiplied. Australia, Egypt, India, and several Latin American countries use radio to improve instruction as well as augment the learning process. In Chile the radio school system operated by the Institute of Rural Education serves more than a thousand rural schools, both public and private, with a variety of lessons by air.[16] Similar radio courses in Middle East countries provide widespread instruction in public health, agriculture, and in reading and writing.

Impressive evidence of the effect of radio broadcasting has been noted in Turkey.[17] It was found that villages distant from a road but with many radios were much more developed, and more eager for development, than villages near a road but lacking radios.

There was more travel by villagers and more visits by outsiders, when a village far from a road (15 or more kilometers) had many radios, than when villages were near a road but had no radios. Travel to and from these villages was determined, not by ease of transport, but by the channels of communications that had been established. Villages near a road but without radios

[15] Wilbur Schramm and Gerald F. Winfield, "New Uses of Mass Communication for the Promotion of Economic and Social Development," *United Nations Conference on the Application of Science and Technology for the Benefit of the Less Developed Areas* (Government Printing Office, 1962), Vol. 12, p. 17.

[16] Hernan Poblete Varas, "Communications and Audio-Visual Systems in Rural Education" (summary of paper for United Nations Conference on the Application of Science and Technology, Geneva, 1962), pp. 1–2.

[17] Paul S. Shapiro, "Development Choices between Transport and Communications," in Edwin T. Haefele (ed.), *Relating Transport to National Policy* (Brookings Institution, 1968).

were substantially less modern. Wherever there were many radios, people had more knowledge about what went on in their village and were more willing to undertake community projects. The presence of radio was more highly associated with attitudes considered prerequisites for development than was the presence of roads.

Along with its ability to involve the listener, radio can reach a large number of people with great speed. The point can be illustrated by a hypothetical example, showing the possible payoff from a large-scale program of rural radio for Indian farmers.

An agricultural extension worker traveling by bicycle may be able to visit two villages a day and talk to 25 people for an hour in each village. In a week he might cover 12 villages and be heard by 300 people. If he were to broadcast once a day through a local station serving 100 villages, his coverage would be greatly multiplied. If 100 sets were tuned in per village and 4 people listened per set, a total of 40,000 people could be reached. During a six-day period of daily broadcasts, therefore, one instructor could provide 240,000 man-hours of instruction, compared to 300 man-hours by bicycle. The radio instruction would have the added merit of being cumulative for those who tuned in daily, whereas personal visits would be at infrequent intervals.

Suppose instruction involved early planting techniques, and the knowledge gained enabled 10 percent of the farmers contacted by each method to increase their yields 50 percent. Of the farmers contacted by bicycle during a week's period, 30 would increase their output; of those listening to the radio, 4,000 would. If the average farmer was producing 1,200 pounds of rice per year, those contacted by bicycle would produce an additional 18,000 pounds. Farmers listening to the radio broadcast would produce an additional yield of 2.4 million pounds.

At 10 cents per pound, the value realized by producers from the additional production accomplished through radio instruction might be on the order of $240,000, and the cost of the added inputs would probably be no more than one-fourth this amount. The sum spent for a week of farm radio programs would be insignificant. Broadcasting costs per hour would be only a few hundred dollars, and even if the cost of radio receivers were allocated to the farm broadcasts alone, costs would be only $80,000. The alternative of training large numbers of agents and paying the necessary transport to enable them to contact the same number of farmers would involve far more time and money.

The significance of the new communications media lies not simply in a specific message transmitted and acted upon, but in the creation of new attitudes and perspectives. What was discovered in Turkey has been noted also in Northern Thailand, where Peace Corps volunteers reported that by the attitudes of people they could tell immediately on entering a village whether or not it had a radio. It is equally apparent, after talking to enthusiastic listeners in Indian villages, that the effects of radio can be "quite independent of its programming"; that for India, in many ways, "the medium is the message."[18]

Communication Potentials for India

There is strong indication that both agriculture and education in Indian villages would be enhanced if ideas and information were moving by radio or TV rather than by bullock carts and mud tracks. But experimentation is needed to find out more about relative costs and impacts, and this could be initiated by some shifting of Fourth Plan allocations for transport and communications to put more emphasis on the latter. For at the margin it appears likely that furthering rural communications stands a better chance of making an impact than the lowest priority transport projects. For fifteen years the stakes have been on building better railways as well as main intercity highways, and the results have generally been impressive. But the side effects have been to bypass a large percentage of the people, to

[18] Marshall McLuhan, *Understanding Media: The Extensions of Man* (McGraw-Hill Book Co., 1964), p. 266.

handicap agriculture, and to neglect important links between agriculture and industry. This imbalance needs to be corrected.

The communications revolution that is offering new ways of transporting information should not be permitted to duplicate these patterns by concentrating on cities and neglecting the hinterlands. Fortunately, by their nature neither TV nor radio follows the restricted paths of road and rail. Some diffusion to rural areas will be inevitable, but planning to assure it will be more effective. To make any notable progress will require specific efforts to equip villages with receivers, to design programs especially for the rural sector, and to assess the results on an experimental basis. Just as a shift is taking place within the transport budget toward village access roads, there should be a further shift of Fourth Plan emphasis from intercity transport to rural-urban communications. If only 5 percent of transport allocations were to be shifted to radio and television, some $200 million could be made available over the five-year period. This would pay for all local currency costs and would redirect resources from marginal transport projects that promise limited economic impact to telecommunications projects that hold out the possibility of a major breakthrough. For the fact is that for the first time the barriers of distance that separate most Indians from the mainstream of economic and social progress could conceivably be surmounted overnight.

If the decision to step up communications involved only domestic resources, the decision could be easily made. But greater emphasis on telephone, radio, and television would mean a substantial increase in foreign exchange requirements. Thus the question that remains to be answered is what magnitude of resources will be needed to bring the total transport and communications program into line with the technological revolution, and what help can be expected from the outside.

CHAPTER VI

Financing a Transport and Communications Breakthrough

INDIA IS FACED WITH the formidable task of modernizing its railways and ports, constructing a network of intercity highways, building new systems of local transport for agriculture, and exploiting the educational possibilities of radio and television. At the same time, traffic congestion in the big cities and the stagnation of half a million small villages point to the need for channeling population growth into a more satisfactory national pattern of urban settlement, using new transport and communications facilities to reverse the current trends.

Efforts to make modern transport and communications technology more responsive to Indian development goals will require a change in direction and substantial help from the outside in both capital transfers and technical assistance. These requirements seem counter to the climate in donor nations, where foreign assistance efforts are flagging and where there are growing signs of disillusionment over aid efforts to date. But clearly the advance of technology demands increasingly sophisticated equipment, and these demands will have to be met if India is to benefit from the innovations that are the principal means of overcoming deficiencies.

Foreign Exchange Requirements

Foreign exchange requirements to meet planned transport targets during the Fourth Plan period are extremely heavy. Dredging equipment, tugs, barges, cranes, and locomotives are needed at the major ports. Improvements are especially urgent at Madras and Marmagoa, where expanded capacity is needed to facilitate the export of iron ore to Japan and Europe. Road transport development depends on imported materials and components for the manufacture of roadbuilding equipment and for the expansion of motor vehicle production. The Indian railways need diesel locomotives, components for coaches and wagons, signal and communications systems, and equipment for electrification. Telecommunications are creating additional new demands for electronic supplies and manufacturing capacity.

The total foreign exchange bill for transport during the Fourth Plan is estimated to be approximately $850 million, including nearly $500 million for the railways, $100 million for shipping, and $80 million for ports. An additional $100 million of new investment is planned for commercial aircraft and aeronautical communications equipment, while communications by telephone and radio may add at least $75 million to import requirements even at the present low rate of expansion. The expanded programs suggested in this study for rural access roads, truck production, transistor radios, and experimental television would require further funds.

An estimated $250 million of the programmed public sector investments will be taken care of by previous commitments of foreign aid through the World Bank, AID, and others, with a balance of over $600 million remaining to be financed. Public sector requirements, however, are only part of the total. The public and private sectors combined ran up a total annual import bill of $250 million for transport in 1964, which was about 10 percent of all Indian imports.

These requirements have to be viewed not simply in relation to the drain on foreign exchange but in terms of how the resulting transport improvements may increase the net availability of foreign exchange, either by increasing export earnings or by reducing dependence on imports. Improvements in transport to permit the delivery of fertilizers and other farm inputs, for example, will ultimately increase agricultural production and reduce the need for food purchases from abroad. These purchases now average $500 million a year. Improved port and rail facilities may help to realize the projected 25 million tons of high-grade iron ore exports per year. And reduction in transport cost can promote overseas sales of Indian manufacturers by reducing production costs.

The three most important exports are tea, jute manufactures, and cotton textiles. Together they accounted for 44 percent of all export earnings in the Third Plan period. (See Table VI–1.) Trade in these items, which has been shifting from rail to road to take advantage of the speed and flexibility of the truck, can benefit from further improvements in road transport. Other exports that move in significant volume and that depend largely on road transport include sugar, vegetable oils, tobacco, hides, and skins. In addition, exports of iron, manganese, mica, and a wide variety of manufactured goods are dependent on high performance by the railways and ports. Increases in train capacity plus port mechanization will be an important means of exploiting mineral resources.

In the area of invisibles, the expenditure of foreign exchange for Indian transport can also help to achieve a net improvement in the balance of payments. Air passenger services in particular can earn tourist dollars. The number of foreign tourists in India has expanded eight-fold in a decade, and currently India is earning approximately $50 million per year from tourism. With improvements in facilities, including transportation, the present inflow of tourist traffic could be substantially increased.

The shortage of internal transport has limited the tourist potential. Extension of the air network is an urgent need because of the long distances between cities. Seventy percent of all tourists arrive in India by air, and availability of connections by Indian Airlines Corporation would promote longer visits and additional travel within the country. Since roads for bus and passenger car travel are nearly everywhere inadequate, building tourist airstrips would permit more people to visit remote places

TABLE VI–1.   *Major Imports and Exports during the Third Plan Period*

Commodity	Millions of U.S. dollars[a]	Percentage distribution
Imports		
Machinery	3,799	29.1
Cereals and other food grains	2,169	16.6
PL 480 food grains	(1,783)	(13.7)
Iron and steel	1,035	7.9
Mineral fuels, lubricants	893	6.9
Transport equipment	738	5.7
Nonferrous metals	602	4.6
Raw cotton (including linters)	573	4.4
Chemicals	369	2.8
Fertilizers	337	2.6
Other imports	2,524	19.3
Total imports	13,039	100.0[b]
Exports		
Jute manufactures	1,682	21.0
Tea	1,292	16.1
Cotton goods	554	6.9
Iron ore	392	4.9
Oilcakes	332	4.2
Fruits and vegetables	323	4.0
Tobacco	204	2.6
Sugar	189	2.4
Spices	183	2.3
Other exports	2,857	35.6
Total exports (including re-exports)	8,008	100.0

Source: Government of India, Planning Commission, *Fourth Five Year Plan: A Draft Outline* (1966), p. 102.

a. Conversion rate: 1 rupee = 21 cents.

b. Column does not add to 100 because of rounding.

not accessible by surface transport. But a larger "package" of facilities will have to be provided, including improved hotels and restaurants, if India is to take advantage of expanding world travel to exploit its many historic attractions and excellent winter weather.

Shipping is another area in which India's foreign exchange position might be improved. At the end of the Third Plan, Indian-owned ships (coastal vessels as well as the overseas merchant fleet) totaled less than half the target of two million tons recommended by India's Shipping Policy Committee two decades ago. Indian ships carry less than 10 percent of the country's overseas freight. Virtually all petroleum imports are being carried by foreign tankers and most of the PL 480 wheat not moved by American ships comes to India in foreign tramps. With the foreign exchange cost of Indian ocean freight amounting to about half as much per year as United States aid to India, there are strong pressures to develop a more effective Indian merchant marine.

However India may move to increase its foreign exchange earnings through improved transport and by import substitution, very large volumes of imported equipment and components will be needed to effect the necessary changes, and a significant part of the bill will have to be financed by foreign loans and other assistance.

The Aid Picture

The United States, the World Bank, and the International Development Association have together provided $1.3 billion of loans and grants to India for transport development during the past decade. World Bank and IDA loans have constituted close to two-thirds of the outside support for the Indian transport system. The Bank itself, as of June 1965, had allocated nearly three-quarters of all its loans to India (the Bank's largest borrower) to transport projects.

Of the total transport aid funds available from all major sources since partition, approximately 60 percent has been for the railways, 30 percent for road transport, 7 percent for ports, and 3 percent for aviation. (See Table VI–2.) The object of World Bank lending was initially the acquisition of locomotives and rail cars, and later the purchase of materials and components for their indigenous manufacture. IDA loans went to road construction and equipment for manufacturing motor vehicles. One

TABLE VI–2.   *Foreign Aid for Indian Transport, 1954–1964*

Transport mode	United States[a]	World Bank[b]	International Development Association[c]	Total
	Millions of dollars			
Railways	304	379	130	813
Road transport	158	. . .	250	408
Highways	(42)[d]		(60)	(102)
Vehicles	(116)		(190)[e]	(306)
Ports	6	64	18	88
Civil aviation	28	6	. . .	34
Aircraft	(25)	(6)		(31)
Airports	(3)			(3)
Miscellaneous	8	. . .	. . .	8
Total	504	449	398	1,351
Percent of total aid	37	33	29	100[f]
	Percentages			
Railways	60	85	33	60
Road transport	31	. . .	63	30
Ports	1	14	5	7
Civil aviation	6	1	. . .	3
Miscellaneous	2	. . .	. . .	. . .
Total	100	100	100[f]	100

Sources: 1954–63 U.S. data from the Agency for International Development; 1964 U.S. data from AID, *Operations Report (Data as of June 1964)* (1965), pp. 32, 104, and the Export-Import Bank Information Office; World Bank (or International Bank for Reconstruction and Development) data from "Statement of Loans" (processed; IBRD, September 1965); and IDA data from "Statement of Development Credits" (processed; IBRD, September 1965).

a. 1954–64.
b. 1949–June 1965.
c. 1961–June 1965.
d. A PL 480 loan of 200 million rupees for national highway construction.
e. Comprises a $90 million credit of 1964 and a $100 million credit of 1965 made available for imports by firms producing commercial vehicles, automotive components, and electrical and construction equipment. The entire amount of these two credits was included in view of the fact that the bulk of the $190 million was to be used for highway transport purposes.
f. Does not total 100 because of rounding.

IDA credit helped to finance half of India's Third Plan national highway program.[1]

Most loans for transport from the United States have been for the Indian railways, including importation of locomotives, steel,

---

[1] IDA loans have provided financing on soft terms that create less balance-of-payments pressure, with credits usually extended for a term of fifty years, including a grace period of ten years and a service charge of less than one percent annually on the balance outstanding.

construction equipment, and traffic control devices. No United States loans have been made specifically for roads, but a third of the transport loans to India from the Agency for International Development and its predecessors have been for automotive manufacturing equipment and motor vehicle components and materials. India has also acquired road construction machinery with non-project loan funds. In the aviation field, most United States funding has been Export-Import Bank credits for the purchase of aircraft. Altogether, the transport sector has accounted for about 16 percent of United States dollar project loans to India.

The task of increasing these sources of financial support for transport runs into difficulties beyond the growing reluctance of the creditor nations. For unless relatively short-term high-interest loans can be supplemented by either long-term loans of the IDA type or outright grants, India will confront an insoluble problem of debt repayment. Outstanding public and publicly-guaranteed indebtedness with a maturity of one year and over rose from $300 million in 1955 to well over $5 billion in 1967.[2] As a consequence, the amount of gross foreign aid that can be counted as net capital assistance has been substantially reduced. In the Fourth Plan, $5 billion of foreign assistance would yield only about half this amount in net assistance.

The time is particularly appropriate for a larger program of foreign assistance to exploit the development potentials of transport and communications. For the first time the Indian railways have achieved a comfortable margin of capacity over demand, so that attention can now be given to a comprehensive attack on the transport system as a whole. Moreover, the Fourth Plan order of priorities has given new direction to the transport program by its emphasis on rural development, food production, and export promotion. Since the Report on Transport Policy and Coordination, too, there has emerged a clearer picture of transport requirements and of the shifts in emphasis that are needed to meet them. In addition, a wider choice of technology is

[2] International Bank for Reconstruction and Development, *Annual Report, 1964–65* (1965), p. 57.

now available to permit systems of movement that make the most effective use of all types of transport, and there is a more general understanding among policy makers of the need to tie transport more closely to specific development goals. In this more favorable atmosphere, the applications of larger amounts of foreign assistance could focus to advantage on three types of transport improvements that would help to support the development effort. First are projects that complement and support the objectives of other aid programs, particularly transport to assist in overcoming the food crisis. Second are projects that involve two or more methods of transport and that further the objective of transport coordination. Third are demonstration projects or experiments with nonconventional solutions that could lead to new ways of coping with old problems.

Transport and Communications for Food

It has been noted that the most urgent requirement in the transport sector is an all-out attack on rural isolation. The limited results of earlier efforts to provide all-weather access to the villages through the Community Development Program are understandable. Transport was less important to agriculture then, because the other elements of more productive farming were still absent. There was no fertilizer, improved seed, or other inputs for intensive cultivation, and there were no trucks. There were also no support prices and government purchasing programs to provide assurance that the cost of growing more would eventually be recouped. Thus even where roads were built, the conditions necessary to make effective use of them were not present, and many miles of new roads fell into disrepair because of the absence of economic incentives to maintain them.

Under the circumstances, the almost exclusive attention given to main intercity rail and highway routes, and the almost complete disregard of local transport requirements, was probably the wisest choice. Improving farm transport could not command a high priority if resulting output could not be expected to cover the cost. But the decision to support intensive cultivation has altered the situation. An intensive agricultural effort makes improved transport an integral part of agriculture. Fertilizers have to move, together with improved seed; and financial incentives are being made available to encourage the marketing of surplus output. The time now invites a determined drive to get roads built, to make vehicles available, and to establish market centers. The question is how to do these quickly and in ways designed to get the best results.

In Chapter III it was seen that local road improvements have been limited not simply by a lack of state-aid funds but by the lack of local funds to match them. The remedy proposed by the Government of India is the 1967 agreement with the states that during the Fourth Five-Year Plan an allocation of 20 percent of all state highway funds will be made for the improvement of rural market roads. The central government will then match 40 percent of this money. A memorandum from the Planning Commission has outlined the type of work envisioned under this market road program.[3]

State aid for market roads is a step in the right direction, but it still overlooks the fact that the states have limited resources for road work. The allocation of 20 percent of state funds for local roads will amount to only about $20 million per year; with central government matching, this will provide only $28 million per year. Additional funds will obviously have to be made available if the road program is to be on an effective scale. How can the resources for such an effort be marshalled?

Road users are one source, but they already carry a heavy tax load. The central government imposes a variety of levies, including import duties on motor vehicles and excise taxes on vehicles, tires, tubes, fuel, and accessories. These taxes now contribute two to four times as much to general revenues as the central government is spending on roads. (See Table VI–3.) This fact—

---

[3] Government of India, Ministry of Transport and Aviation, Memorandum to All State Governments, "Rural-Market Roads," Jan. 19, 1967.

TABLE VI–3. *Road User Tax Revenues and Highway Expenditures, 1950–64*[a]
(In millions of rupees)

Year	Central government			State government		
	Revenue (1)	Expenditures (2)	Ratio (1/2)	Revenue (3)	Expenditures (4)	Ratio (3/4)
1950–51	348.2	86.7	4.02	125.5	293.8	.43
1955–56	455.5	247.3	1.84	258.3	574.4	.45
1960–61	1,070.1	298.0	3.59	549.2	699.6	.79
1963–64	2,023.4	639.3[b]	3.17	1,069.9	811.5	1.32

Sources: Government of India, *Basic Road Statistics of India*, annual issues; and Government of India, Ministry of Finance, *Central and State Budgets*, annual issues.

a. Expenditures include development as well as maintenance expenditures. Cost of collection is not included.

b. This figure was obtained by subtracting state road expenditures from the total road expenditures amounting to 1,450.8 million rupees.

plus the potential benefits from improved roads—suggests a larger allocation of existing user revenues to road purposes, rather than imposition of additional taxes.

Crediting India's Central Road Fund with more of the existing revenues from road user taxes is the place to start. This fund is financed by a small tax levied on the sale of gasoline. Eighty percent of the proceeds are allocated to the states on the basis of their gasoline consumption, and the remainder is used by the central government for special projects of national importance. But as the Committee on Transport Policy and Coordination has noted, most trucks and buses in India are diesels, so their contribution is almost nil. The tax on diesel fuel is not credited to the Road Fund, although the Committee has recommended that this be done. Other taxes on motor vehicles and their operation, now going to the general fund, could also be credited in part to the central roadbuilding fund as a logical means of accelerating the development and modernization of the motor transport system.

Public policy and administrative efficiency, of course, must determine whether or not special taxes levied on road users should be earmarked to pay for highways, but the weight of experience suggests that there are important advantages to this method. There is obvious equity in attempting to exact from the users of certain types of public services the cost of the public works built for their special benefit. This is the way the railways are financed, and to an increasing degree ports and airports. The alternative of relying on the general taxpayer to foot the bill has its drawbacks, especially when there are so many public needs that cannot be priced and that must compete for general tax revenues.

A further advantage of user charges for road financing is that highway development requires long-term planning and programming, and road administrators can benefit from a long-term indication of the revenues that can be committed in advance. The establishment of a relationship between traffic "earnings" and the design and cost of road improvements also introduces economic concepts into road planning and administration and helps reduce some of the political pressures in road location and project priorities. In addition, those who pay the bill know that they will benefit from their taxes through reduced vehicle operating costs, so that the acceptability of such taxes (as in Madras State) is enhanced. And since road transport competes with railways, which price their services, the inclusion of the cost of highways in the price paid for highway services creates a more comparable basis for the allocation of traffic and investments.

While it appears desirable that more of the proceeds of central government user charges should be allocated to roads, in India roads are primarily a state responsibility. The question thus arises whether state taxes could also be relied upon for the additional support needed to build village access roads. A negative answer is indicated by the fact that the states already exact both heavy fees for vehicle registration and high taxes on motor fuel and on passenger and goods movement. It would be unfair, moreover, during a period of rapidly expanding road construction, for today's road users to pay the entire current outlay for roads, which is substantially higher than the annual economic cost. A large part of the current outlay for roads is investment in new facilities that will last for many years, and their cost should be defrayed in part by future as well as current users.

Another factor making further local tax increases undesirable is the small number of motor vehicles operating in India at this stage. Transport's contribution to development will not be furthered by high charges for highways that discourage the use of road investment already made. It is not recommended, therefore, that state taxes on highway users be raised, and it has already been seen that local capacity to pay for public facilities is extremely limited.

Local governments can help to underwrite the very large task of improving village access roads, however, by arrangements that permit the public to recoup some of the benefits from new roads. Just as the cultivator needs credit to buy fertilizer and seed before he can realize the return from intensive cultivation, financial arrangements are needed which will get the roads built and permit local contributions to be made after the economic benefits have been created. What is needed is a revolving fund to pay the initial cost of road construction; this cost, or some part of it, can be returned to the fund through taxes assessed on the land after it has begun producing more.

In other words, an aid program that pays only part of the cost of local roads is not enough. A far more effective program would be to pay 100 percent of the cost initially, with later repayment of part or all of the money into a revolving fund which would be used to finance additional projects as funds were recouped. This repayment could be accomplished over a period of five to ten years, through taxes levied on the owners of property affected by the road improvements.

Along with better roads, trucks that can take advantage of them are needed. In all parts of India a potentially profitable relationship between farmers and urban industry is unexploited. The cities need food and agricultural raw materials and they can provide the villager with fertilizer, tools, equipment, and consumer goods. But the transport links between the two have not been provided to encourage this interchange. Good trucking services are one of the essential components for such a trading relationship.

Where volume and trip length warrant the use of trucks, transport costs will at least be cut in half. More important, in many cases the truck is the only way to move the loads offered or to cover the distances. India in 1964 had 0.5 trucks per 1,000 persons. Except for Pakistan and Ethiopia, this was fewer than any major country. Syria had 2.3 trucks per 1,000 persons, Thailand 2.1, and Japan 35. (Appendix Table 10.) If India were to increase its fleet to only 2 per 1,000 people, or a million trucks, it would need about 750,000 more than it had in 1967. Many of these would be small pickups in local service, for transporting supplies to individual farms and for collecting produce. Larger vehicles would be needed by suppliers of fertilizer and for over-the-road transport of consumer goods and consolidated loads of produce moving to market centers.

In addition to roads and trucks, a target of 20,000 local storage units, rice mills, and other processing plants has been set for the Fourth Plan. The road improvement program and the choice of sites for market towns will provide the best guidance in locating these facilities. Finally, rural transport will need to be supplemented by improved communications, as part of the effort to close the rural-urban information gap.

The magnitude of the task of overcoming distance suggests the need for a special foreign aid effort. And to make best use of aid, a transport and communications program for food is needed, to be carried out cooperatively by the Ministries of Transport, Communications, and Agriculture.

The principal foreign exchange costs in such a program would be for expanding production of trucks, roadbuilding machinery, radio transmitters, and transistor radio receivers, and for extending television to rural areas. Parts and components to achieve truck production targets would involve some $429 million of imports, 80 percent for one-ton trucks, and the rest for over-the-road vehicles. (See Table VI–4.) Radio sets would involve another $270 million. This figure assumes that half the goal of 100 million radio sets would be achieved in the Fourth Plan (only 5 million sets were made available in 1966). To reach the 50 million set target, half the transistorized receivers might have to be imported, and the other half produced locally with imported parts, involving an average foreign exchange component of 20 percent. Import of sets may be required in the

TABLE VI–4.   *Transport and Communications Program for Agriculture*
A.   Foreign Exchange Requirements

Purpose	Total, 1966	1971 target	Foreign exchange requirements (in millions of dollars)	Basis of estimate
Television			$11.0	
Receiving sets	5,000	50,000	9.0	$200 per set, $1 million per
Operating stations	1	5	2.0	center, 50 percent foreign exchange
Truck production				
Trucks (thousands)	255	1,000ᵃ	$429.0	20 percent foreign exchange, + 10 percent allowance for replacements
Radio			$300.0	
Receiving sets (millions)	5	50	270.0	$10 per set, half imported, 20 percent
Maintenance			30.0	foreign exchange for domestic output
Road construction equipment			$37.5	One-tenth of local road construction costs, 50 percent foreign exchange
Total foreign exchange costs			$777.5	

a. Eighty percent of the total are one-ton farm trucks at $2,000; the remainder are over-the-road trucks at $5,000.

B.   Estimated Costs of a Five-Year Local Road Program[a]
(Intensive Agricultural Areas)

Type of improvement	Miles	Cost per mile (in dollars)	Total cost (in millions of dollars)
IAA roads to be surfaced (one-half)	42,000	4,000	168
IAA roads to be improved but not surfaced	42,000	2,000	84
New roads for IAA's	84,000	6,000	504
Total improvement program	168,000	4,500	756
Maintenance program	168,000	500	168[b]
Grand total			924

a. There are 420,000 existing local rural roads in all of India; 84,000 of these are assumed to be in Intensive Agricultural Areas.

b. Total for the five years includes no expenditure for the first year and assumes that one-fifth of the system will be completed each year.

short run, because of the time lag in expanding local production capacity and the relatively low cost of imported sets, as discussed in Chapter V. There would be additional import requirements for replacement batteries and maintenance parts.[4] The construction of transmitters to extend broadcast coverage and to tailor programs to local needs would involve additional foreign investment funds.

To expand television by adding four transmitters and by extending TV coverage through school and community TV centers would require equipment and supplies with about a 50 percent foreign exchange content, but the total would be very modest. Imports for transmitters, 45,000 receivers, and the establishment of four new TV centers would total $11 million during the Fourth Plan. The TV network would also require imports of expendable equipment and materials for program production.

Altogether, the foreign exchange costs of a transport and communications program aimed at agriculture and rural development would total three-quarters of a billion dollars over a five-

[4] Based on data from the Government of India, Ministry of Information and Broadcasting, "Report of the Committee on Broadcasting and Information Media on Broadcasts for Rural Areas" (mimeographed, 1965).

year period. The sale of imported equipment by the government would create a rupee equivalent sufficient, with matching funds, to support the proposed rural market road program. The local costs of storage units, processing plants, and communications programming might also be covered.

The local road program for improvements and new construction of 168,000 miles in the Intensive Agricultural Areas is estimated to require nearly a billion dollars over a five-year period. (Table VI–4.) Since this represents the major part of the transport and communications program, the most practical procedure would be to deposit in the Central Road Fund the entire amount of the local currency made available from the sale of imported equipment to be allocated to the states for roads. The stipulation could be made that part of this money might be used for ancillary facilities such as storage and other market center requirements.

In carrying out the roadbuilding program, the central government would retain one percent of the fund to defray the costs of organizing, administering, and conducting the program, including the preparation of standards and instructions to guide state and local participants. The balance would be distributed among the states on the basis of population and area, to be deposited in revolving state road funds and matched by state contributions already agreed to. This matching money would help to cover the costs of maintaining the new road system. Conditions stipulated for the use of these funds would include the designation of eligible routes in Intensive Agricultural Areas and repayment by local governments into the state revolving fund of a part of the cost of local roads.

The public works department at district level would own, maintain, and make available the roadbuilding equipment and machinery acquired through the aid program. Regulated markets, cooperatives, or other distributors of agricultural supplies would be assisted in purchasing trucks through appropriate credit arrangements.

Central, state, and local governments would all share the responsibility for market road planning and financing. The 123 districts included in the IAAs are the logical state subdivisions to provide technical and logistic services and to supervise the local road program, while the 1,444 community development blocks in the Intensive Agricultural Areas appear to be the appropriate units to help integrate local village plans and carry out the work.

To a limited extent transport planning through local government has already been successfully accomplished in India, and local units have shown an awareness of the need for better transport and a willingness to participate. In Wardha district of Maharashtra, for example, 37 market centers were chosen as growth points around which to build a district development plan. It became apparent at an early stage that accessibility was the highest priority.[5] One-third of all Third Plan investments recommended by the representative body of Wardha district (the Zila Parishad) were road projects. The popular desire for better roads is indicated by the fact that more funds were allocated to this purpose than to agricultural production, soil conservation, irrigation, education, and health combined. The road plan was based on linking up the market centers, connecting Wardha with neighboring districts, and developing areas where resource potentials were attractive. A total of 190 miles of approach roads were included, plus 160 miles of roads for access to resources.[6]

An important side effect of a local road program to support agriculture is to provide jobs and income for workers who are only partially or seasonally employed. Much road construction and later maintenance could be done by labor-intensive methods. The program would directly support the Fourth Plan goals of providing more rural purchasing power, to buy both consumer goods and inputs for commercial agriculture.

[5] The plan was based on a study by the Gokhale Institute of Politics and Economics, Poona.

[6] Information from Government of India, Ministry of Community Development and Cooperation, Nov. 28, 1964.

Aid for Coordination and Experimentation

In addition to the proposed special program for transport and communications to increase food supplies, it was noted earlier that $850 million of foreign exchange would be required to carry out the official Fourth Plan proposals for rail, water, and air transport. Half the total is planned for the railways, but in the light of rapidly changing technology special attention is needed to avoid unnecessary or uneconomic investments in this area. This means assuring that rail modernization is limited to areas where the railways can operate effectively in the long run. It is also important that appropriate programs for abandonment of uneconomic branch lines are pressed, and that necessary rate increases are imposed on short-haul traffic and small shipments that now fail to pay even their direct costs.

A further possibility for reducing capital requirements on the railways lies in concentrating on communications facilities to achieve better use of existing equipment. Over half the railway requirements for foreign exchange in the Fourth Plan is for rolling stock. Improved communications could help locate and direct the movement of equipment to reduce time losses, meet customer needs, and put idle wagons to work. A more rapid changeover to diesel power is another step that would increase the utilization of rolling stock.

Integrated freight transport using containers could also be accelerated by the aid program through the acquisition of rail flatcars, motor trucks, and the containers themselves, and through the construction of container terminals. A railway subsidiary might devote full attention to establishing and operating integrated road-rail services, which would ultimately be extended to ocean transport and air cargo services. Physical integration rather than regulatory controls will provide the hoped-for coordination of transport in India.

A preliminary step in this direction would be a survey of potential container traffic to identify the routes to be served, the equipment to be purchased, and the highway and rail facilities to be improved. A related survey is needed to determine the prospects and requirements for unit train operations. These heavy train movements would permit substantial economies in mineral traffic, chemicals, and other bulk movements.

Foreign assistance in introducing transport innovations could also have a significant payoff in aviation. The lack of adequate roads in India, the great length of time consumed in long-distance movements, and both the legal and geographic restrictions on surface transport increase the economic advantages of air freight to serve major cities. The potential for increasing air transport's role in long-distance intercity passenger travel should also be explored. Air transport expansion could play an important part in saving time for key personnel, and the use of small planes, including vertical and steep take-off and landing aircraft, may be the most economical method of transporting agricultural technicians.

The assumption that air services are a luxury to be introduced only after the development of ground services is based on a misreading of experience in more developed nations. These nations failed to exploit aviation more aggressively for understandable reasons. One is the comparatively recent appearance of aircraft with versatility and high-performance characteristics. Another is the relatively good surface transport available in the West before the air age began. Moreover, industry location had been determined and distribution techniques well established before aviation entered the picture.

In India the situation is different. Air cargo and passenger services could provide better transport services than are available on the ground, and might produce substantial savings. A broader network of air services for the subcontinent could introduce new methods of doing business, a reduction in inventory requirements, the organization of nationwide enterprises, and a further expansion of tourist travel.

Organizing a More Effective Program

If there is to be a more effective transport program realistically reflecting India's requirements, one of the most obvious needs is for new programming capabilities at the top. The Government of India moved toward a systems approach to transport in 1966, when it created the new Ministry of Transport and Aviation, comprising all transport agencies except the railways. But omission of the railways goes far to cancel the potential impact of this reorganization. Since nearly 90 percent of public investments in transport are road and rail, the separation of these two elements nullifies much of the effort to improve transport decision-making.

Today, with the growing capacity to design and build total systems, the need for an appropriate administrative framework has become obvious. It was concluded by the Committee on Transport Policy and Coordination, however, that assigning all transport responsibilities to a single Ministry of Transport would create "an extremely heavy burden to carry."[7] Hence, although the most effective approach to transport modernization is through investment decisions, these continue to be made independently for road and rail, and no agency is responsible for examining alternatives or combinations that might assure better results.

A Ministry of Transport could be made manageable, as the new United States Department of Transportation is expected to demonstrate, by concentrating its activities on research and policy planning, where the major vacuum now exists. For example, the Indian railways could be operated through a public corporation comparable to the present corporate management of the airlines, thus freeing the Ministry from operating responsibilities. This would give the railways more of the freedom

[7] Government of India, Planning Commission, *Committee on Transport Policy and Coordination: Final Report* (1966), p. 218.

of a commercial enterprise and would permit the Ministry to serve as the architect of a unified transport network designed to make possible the goals of Indian economic development.

A research and policy planning staff in the Transport Ministry would provide the means of analyzing the cost and effectiveness of alternative transport investments, and of assuring satisfactory physical and operating relationships among transport methods now separately planned, built, and operated. Many problems facing Indian transport cannot be given the attention they deserve simply because no agency is responsible for the transport system as a whole.

The absence of central governmental machinery that would permit a comprehensive view of transport is a serious obstacle to selecting transport investments. Almost every major decision involving rail transport has implications for the rest of the transport system, while actions with respect to the development of road transport affect the railways. Often the optimal solution requires action to be taken simultaneously in two or more areas. To ignore these relationships often wastes resources and fails to take maximum advantage of available technology.

In addition to placing responsibility for railway policy in the Ministry of Transport, there is need for a stronger organization for road transport policy. The road transport responsibilities of the central government, as we have seen, should include not only the national highways and the nation's supply of motor vehicles, but technical and financial aid for state and local roads. The contrast in management organization between rail and road transport in India goes a long way toward explaining the poor condition of road transport. There are obvious reasons, of course, why railway administration cannot be duplicated in road transport. Road transport responsibilities are divided between construction of highways and operation of motor vehicles. Highway responsibilities are in turn divided among central, state, and local governments. Road transport functions can be upgraded at the central government level, however, by committing larger amounts of money to research and planning and by establishing a Road Transport Agency in the Ministry of Transport, responsible for national highways, state aid, and vehicle production.

But the relation between the Transport Ministry and the Planning Commission is equally important. It was noted earlier that although transport requirements stem from goals in other sectors, transport decisions are often unrelated to these targets. The task of assuring that plans for transport are viewed in relation to the needs of agriculture or industry, or to energy resources and export promotion policies, is the responsibility of the Planning Commission. The Commission has not been able to concentrate on its major function, however, because it is burdened with technical details which, in the absence of an all-inclusive transport ministry, are left on the Commission's doorstep. The planners are being forced to make technical transport decisions without benefit of research and analysis support, and are without time to carry out their principal policy-making role.

The functions of the Planning Commission are not only to make the transport program goals-oriented, but to explore ways of achieving stated objectives with minimum investment or perhaps through non-transport solutions, and then to assure that resources will be made available for the investments agreed upon. And the Commission should be concerned with the geographic aspects of the development program, which depend heavily on transport capabilities, but so far it has been unable to provide this type of program guidance effectively.

Improvements and innovations in administration are also urgently needed to rationalize transport operations. Attention has been directed in particular to the logic of the railways engaging in truck transport. The establishment of regional transport companies operating all types of transport may eventually provide the answer to the current fragmentation of transport supply. The growing recognition of the need for overall transport policy decisions can be expected to hasten the day when the facilities and operations themselves will also be integrated.

Strengthening investments in the great variety of economic activities that support the transport system is another objective that requires attention if transport is to make its maximum contribution to development. Supporting industries include metals, petroleum refining, tire manufacture, roadbuilding equipment, motor vehicle production, shipbuilding, and the supply of materials and components. Many of these economic activities could be accelerated through greater encouragement of private capital and management services. Increased roadbuilding activity and the reduction of restrictions on motor vehicle use are setting the stage in India for foreign private assistance in a wide variety of supporting services.

Thus far the major share of private investment has gone into such industries as pharmaceuticals, electric goods, iron and steel products, machinery, and machine tools. These types of joint ventures in the transport and communications field could profitably be extended to enable India to supply more of her equipment needs indigenously. Further agreements with foreign firms could accelerate the growth of manufacturing, expand the supply of available capital, augment Indian know-how, and create jobs.

In this regard, Indian transport should benefit from more liberal private loan guarantee programs like that of the United States Agency for International Development. The AID program is designed to tap the very large sums of investment money available through insurance companies and pension funds. United States government guarantees against risks incurred by private investors have already multiplied the capital available for fertilizer plants and other facilities to aid food production. The AID program underwrites foreign-owned as well as United States companies, thus encouraging private investment from all sources. A close partnership of public and private investment could be the means of attracting the large sums that will be necessary to expand domestic production of transport and communications equipment.

CHAPTER VII

Overcoming Distance

IN INDIA, AS IN OTHER developing countries, a key factor in economic development is the rapid growth of the transport burden with rising levels of economic activity. Every increase in national product is accompanied by two to three times as great an increase in the movement of materials. But in the more developed countries, experience indicates that less transportation is needed per unit of national product. And now science and technology have introduced new materials, new processing techniques, substitutes for transport, and new energy resources that can reduce the volume of movement still further. The importance of these trends is that by reducing the resources that have to be devoted to transport per unit of output, relatively more effort can be devoted to directly productive activities. By lessening the nation's transport burdens relative to its accomplishments, India can hope to narrow the gap between its living standards and those of economically more advanced societies.

Currently the transport problems of India are frustrating testimony to the impact of distance on development. The long distances to be covered on the subcontinent have resulted in high costs of carriage, restricted market areas, rural isolation, and failure to make use of available forest, mineral, and agricultural resources. And there is a very wide area, the rural hinterland, in which modern transport has never been provided. Thus, while a given journey may not be long, dependence on the bullock cart in effect makes it long, and the sum of the short spaces that connect India's half million towns and villages with the main urban centers represents a very large mileage and a potentially heavy investment in facilities.

For covering long distances, the railways generally provide satisfactory freight transport. The movements of large volumes of coal and food grains are examples. But for the fast delivery of high-value manufactures, and the accommodation of short hauls and light traffic densities, rail is hardly satisfactory. Railways are even less satisfactory for much of the travel of India's people.

Today there are alternatives, and motor vehicles and airplanes can be expected to carry an increasing proportion of the Indian transport burden. Often a combination of technologies will provide the best answers. In addition, the spatial separation of people may be overcome in part through communications which for some purposes eliminate the problem of distance. But Indian transport policy has not fully caught up with the revolution in transport and telecommunications. The effect has been to retard economic development, and in particular to perpetuate the stagnation of agriculture and rural life. Moreover, in seeking solutions to urgent national problems, public policy in India has not availed itself of the contribution that transport and communications technology can make.

Specifically, the transport and communications system to serve India in the next five to ten years will require a concentration of efforts in eleven major areas:

1. A million miles of improved highways will be required to link the cities and towns and to bridge the gap between rural India and the urban-industrial economy. The most important part of the program is the network of access roads in Intensive Agricultural Areas that comprise about one-fifth of the country. For this purpose about 84,000 miles of new roads will be required to link the villages with market towns, and an equal number of existing roads will need to be improved. Millions of unemployed workers can be engaged in this effort—a transportation-for-food program that will at the same time furnish the

purchasing power, accessibility, and incentives essential to transforming agriculture and rural society.

2. The main system of national highways, still incomplete and mostly one-lane, will have to be selectively improved to permit the free flow of traffic over its principal segments. The central government can assure that interstate truck transport is free to move on the system without being subject to the unnecessary interference of individual states. Financing arrangements for truck purchases are urgently needed. And unless the harassments created by licensing, taxation, and regulatory policies are ended, the resources being allocated to highways may be lost through restrictions imposed on highway use.

3. The rail system will have to be modernized to enable it to concentrate on the specialized services that rail transport will be called upon to perform in the coming decade. Improvements to services already obsolescent need to be avoided. The main rail lines should be equipped to operate unit trains for the movement of bulk commodities, and container trains for expediting door-to-door freight pickup and delivery and interchange among land, water, and air carriers. Integrated land services should be operated by a nation-wide road-rail freight service.

4. At the very least, the railways should be permitted and encouraged to operate their own truck fleets for local pickup and delivery services, for branch line service, and for supplementary over-the-road services. The objective should be the development of regional transport companies using both road and rail equipment.

5. Truck transport capabilities in the private sector are essential to meet the expanding needs of industrialization, commercial agriculture, and rural development. Large numbers of light trucks will have to be supplied for farm use and local delivery services, for agricultural pickup and delivery, and for private over-the-road haulage. The expansion of India's motor vehicle fleet, now among the world's smallest in relation to population, could be a major factor in stimulating development. A million trucks should be available early in the Fifth Plan period

to meet the needs of expanding business and increased food production.

6. Expanded bus systems are also needed, and they should provide nationwide passenger services as well as added capacity for urban transit. Bus transport should be substituted for rail service on low-density lines unable to cover operating expenses.

7. An expanded air transport system should be provided to speed travel of business executives, government officials, and technicians, and to support increased tourism. Aircraft can also help to support rural development programs in health, agriculture, and related services. The great distances separating urban centers also suggest the economic desirability of all-cargo air service to meet the needs of major cities.

8. Road and air transport as well as telecommunications can help make possible new patterns of urban settlement capable of stemming the tide toward the big city. These new tools for dispersal need to be augmented by providing incentives for the growth of medium-sized cities and by discouraging further congestion of already overcrowded metropolitan concentrations. As the period of major migration from farm to city gets under way, India should be armed with a national plan for a new urban geography.

9. Within the existing congested cities, the trend toward transport motorization will continue, and the problems it brings will increase. But better housing and public services of all kinds should not be sacrificed for costly transport solutions. The first requirement is to introduce the measures necessary to avoid future unmanageable traffic. The effort should be made, through land-use planning, to prevent further overcrowding and excessive densities, and to reduce unnecessary movement and undesirable industrial concentrations.

10. The foreign exchange requirements of transport are large, but so are the possibilities that transport can earn foreign exchange. Better rural transport can help substitute domestic production for food imports. Transport facilities will have to be built to overcome the distances that separate forest and mineral re-

sources from industry, and from markets abroad. New rail lines and port mechanization will have to be provided, and new roads to forest areas. Air transport can help expand earnings from international travel, and investment in domestic shipping could reduce the foreign exchange costs of overseas trade.

11. A greatly expanded network of radio and television coverage is required to improve the communications functions now poorly performed by the transport system. A desirable immediate target for transistor radios would be 50 million sets. Television offers even greater opportunities for annihilating distance at reasonable cost. Better communications could help to improve rural education, introduce new farming techniques, and disseminate information on health, community development, and agricultural marketing. Substituting communications for transport could pay off heavily in more effective technical assistance. Ten percent of the present transport budget shifted to telecommunications could have far-reaching development impact.

In every country, the task of improving transport and communications is largely a problem of applying the fruits of science and technology, of matching them with innovations in organization and procedure, and of selecting the course that promises the most significant net contribution to development. For every country or area that seeks to hasten its development, the important lesson is that rural isolation, ignorance, traditionalism, and lack of incentive are to a major degree the products of poor transport and the inability to communicate. India's frustrations stem in no small measure from the impossibility, uncertainty, slowness, or high costs of overcoming the distances that separate people, goods, and ideas. The tools are now available to make major inroads on the age-old problems of immobility and inaccessibility.

The major impediment is not technology, but rather the difficulty of organizing and financing a goals-oriented program, as distinguished from individual transport projects often too narrowly conceived to attain the maximum development impact. A transport and communications program designed to help expand the supply of food is an example of the kind of departure that is necessary. A program that includes roads and vehicles, storage and processing, radio and television, should be added to the overall effort to introduce water, fertilizer, and other inputs into an intensive agricultural effort.

India's problems focus attention on a world-wide need for more effective arrangements for providing the funds and technical help required to accelerate economic and social development through transport and communications. There are no adequate world-wide channels for the exchange of information on the economic development aspects of transport, and on the experience of various countries struggling with similar problems. No large-scale research and educational efforts are sponsored by the United Nations in this field, as they are in agriculture, health, and industry. There are no major efforts to marshall the necessary financial resources. What is needed in transport is the comprehensive assistance that typifies the operations carried out in agriculture by the Food and Agriculture Organization, or in health by the World Health Organization. Without an appropriate organizational framework, all countries are handicapped by the absence of information, the disorganization of research and development efforts, the shortage of trained personnel, the needless repetition of errors, and failure to profit from successful transport policies and programs elsewhere.

A Center for Transport and Development, affiliated with and serving the needs of the United Nations, should be added to the existing system of technical organizations to provide the necessary focal point for world-wide efforts to relate transport solutions to economic and social problems. In view of the totality of the transport system and its pervasive influence on development, the absence of an appropriate transport program is inconsistent with the objectives of international cooperation and development. For it is now abundantly clear that transport cannot be looked upon merely as an isolated problem, but is an integral part of other efforts to narrow the gap between rich countries and poor.

The organization of a global effort to strengthen transport links will have to be accompanied by larger transfers of capital than are now provided through conventional aid channels. An approach to more realistic levels of support was the decision by the United Nations General Assembly to initiate in 1968 a new United Nations Capital Development Fund, to supplement other sources of assistance with grants and long-term low-interest loans. The time is approaching when a specific assessment levied on all of the more developed nations will be essential to supplying the sums needed to effect a global revolution in transport and communications. The problem affects not just the one out of six people who are Indians, but the five out of six for whom distance and isolation go a long way toward explaining poverty and stagnation.

Appendix Tables

TABLE A–1.   *Public Expenditures for Transport Development in the First Three Five-Year Plans*

(In crores of rupees)[a]

Purpose	Actual expenditures		Estimated expenditures
	First Plan	Second Plan	Third Plan
Railways	260	814	1,323
Roads and road transport	143	254	472
Inland water transport	. . .[b]	1	3
Ports and harbors	27	32	91
Shipping	18	55	41
Civil air transport	29	42	50
Other transport	. . .[b]	6	10
Total transport expenditures	477	1,204	1,990
Total development expenditures	1,960	4,672	8,631

Sources: Government of India, Planning Commission, *Selected Plan Statistics* (February 1963), pp. 33, 123. Third Plan expenditures are from Government of India, Planning Commission, *Fourth Five Year Plan: A Draft Outline* (1966), p. 297. See Table A–3 for the total public expenditures in the Third and Fourth plans.

a. One crore = 10,000,000. The official rate of exchange was 4.7 rupees to 1 U.S. dollar until 1966, when the rupee was devalued to 7.5 per dollar.

b. Included in civil air transport.

TABLE A–2.   *The Transport Investment Picture: Public and Private Sectors*

(In crores[a] of rupees and percent)

Selected figures and comparisons	First Plan	Second Plan	Third Plan	Total
Total investment in the economy	3,360	6,750	11,700	21,810
Investment in transport	577	1,399	2,266	4,242
Transport as percent of total	17.2	20.7	19.4	19.4
Railroad transport as percent of all transport	37.4	51.8	58.4	53.3
Road transport as percent of all transport	42.3	28.7	31.2	31.9

Source: Data are from the Government of India, Transport Division of the Planning Commission.

a. See Table A–1, note *a*, for an explanation of this measure.

TABLE A–3. *Outlays for Transportation and Other Purposes in India's Third and Fourth Five-Year Plans*

(In crores[a] of rupees)

Purpose	Third Plan	Percent	Fourth Plan	Percent
Transportation	1,990	23	2,730	17
Communications	126	2	280	2
Agriculture[b]	1,103	13	2,410	15
Irrigation and power	1,919	22	2,994	19
Industry	1,955	23	4,306	27
Social services	1,422	17	3,210	20
Others	116	1	70	. . .[c]
Total	8,631	100[d]	16,000	100

Source: Government of India, Planning Commission, *Fourth Five Year Plan: A Draft Outline* (1966), pp. 72–74.
a. See Table A–1, note *a*, for an explanation of this measure.
b. Includes community development programs.
c. Percent is 0.4.
d. Because of rounding, total exceeds 100.

TABLE A–4. *Selected Targets of the Fourth Plan*

Sector	1970–71	Percentage increase over 1965–66
National income (in crores of 1965–66 rupees)[a]	29,500	48
Industrial production (1956 = 100)	306	69
Food grains (million tons)	120	33
Nitrogenous fertilizers (million tons)	2	233
Phosphatic fertilizers (million tons)	1	567
Steel ingots (million tons)	11.7	89
Petroleum products (million tons)	20	102
Iron ore (million tons)	54	135
Coal (million tons)	106	51
Power—installed capacity (million kilowatts)	20	96
Rural electrification (number of villages)	110,000	110
Students in schools (millions)	97.5	44
Major irrigation works (million acres)	9	64
Number of telephones (millions)	1.5	72

Source: Government of India, Planning Commission, *Fourth Five Year Plan: A Draft Outline* (1966), pp. 39, 40, 47, 49, 53, 60–61.
a. See Table A–1, note *a*, for an explanation of this measure.

TABLE A–5. *The Indian Transport System, 1965*

Basic transport facilities	Quantity
Highways (kilometers)	958,000
Surfaced	284,000
Unsurfaced	674,000
Railway routes (kilometers)	58,276
Broad gauge	28,440
Meter gauge	25,510
Narrow gauge	4,326
Pipelines (kilometers)	1,572
Inland waterways (kilometers)	13,500
Airports (number of units)	86 (4 jet)
Major port capacity (million tons)	57

Transportation equipment	Number of units
Railway locomotives[a]	15,536
Passenger coaches	23,863
Freight cars	337,424
Motor vehicles	718,000
Trucks	255,000
Buses	73,000
Passenger cars	390,000
Aircraft	85[b]
Merchant fleet (thousand GRT)	
Coastal vessels	1,218
Overseas vessels	323

Sources: Government of India, Planning Commission, *Fourth Five Year Plan: A Draft Outline* (1966), p. 294; number of cars from the International Road Federation, and other equipment figures from the Planning Commission.

a. For broad gauge only.

b. 1960–61.

TABLE A–6.   *Goods Transported by Truck from Delhi to Bombay*[a]

Commodity	Tons	Average haul (in kilometers)
Fruit and vegetables	5,951	323
Food grains	3,683	324
Textiles	3,366	972
Oil	2,515	477
Iron and steel	2,202	666
Fodder	1,919	160
Machinery	1,837	1,296
Medicine and chemicals	1,600	970
Ghee and vegetable oils	1,540	636
Provisions	1,363	843
Sugar	1,343	534
Building materials	1,240	270
Cotton	1,225	677
Livestock	1,095	1,298
Other commodities	11,759	840
Total and average	42,638	671

a. Part of a seven-day survey made in 1963 by the Government of India, Ministry of Transport and Communication, Department of Transport, in connection with the World Bank Coal Transport Study on routes comprising 8,000 miles of the 15,000-mile national highway system.

TABLE A–7.   *Growth of Transport and Gross National Product in Japan, 1956–65*

Sector	1956	1965	Percent increase
Intercity freight traffic			
(billion ton-kilometers)	*102*	*197*	93
Railways	48	58	21
Coastal shipping	43	82	91
Trucks	11	49	346
Others	. . .	8	. . .
Capital investment			
(million dollars)[a]	*381*	2,891	659
Railways	218	1,971	804
Road	163	920	464
Motor vehicles in use			
(thousands)	*1,008*	6,641	559
Trucks	759	4,352	473
Automobiles	173	2,034	1,076
Buses	37	100	170
Others	38	154	305
Gross national product (in			
constant billion dollars)[a]	29.7[b]	67.6[c]	*128*

Sources: Data supplied by Saburo Okita, Japan Economic Research Center, Tokyo, Japan, 1966. GNP figures from Government of Japan, Economic Planning Agency, *Annual Report of National Income Statistics, 1967* (1967); and Government of Japan, Economic Planning Agency, *National Account Statistics Quarterly*, No. 13 (September 1966).

a. At the conversion rate of $1.00 = 360 yen.

b. In constant billion yen, 10,701.2.

c. In constant billion yen, 24,346.6.

TABLE A–8.   *U.S. Intercity Freight Traffic, 1960–65*[a]

(In billions of ton-miles)

Year	Railways	Trucks	Pipelines	Great Lakes, rivers, and canals	Air	Total
1950	597	173	129	164	.3	1,063
1960	579	286	229	130	.8	1,314
1961	570	297	233	210	.9	1,310
1962	600	309	238	223	1.3	1,372
1963	629	332	253	234	1.3	1,450
1964	666	350	268	250	1.5	1,536
1965[b]	705	370	310	256	1.9	1,643
			Percentages			
1950	56	16	12	16	· · ·	100
1960	44	22	17	17	0.1	100
1961	44	23	18	16	0.1	100
1962	44	23	17	16	0.1	100
1963	43	23	17	16	0.1	100
1964	44	23	17	16	0.1	100
1965[b]	43	23	19	16	0.1	100

Source: Transportation Association of America, *Transportation Facts and Trends* (3d ed.; TAA, 1966), p. 7.
a. Includes mail and express.
b. Preliminary.

TABLE A–9.   *Trends in Soviet Transport, 1950–65*

(In billions of metric ton-kilometers)

Year	Rail	River	Domestic sea	All trucks	Oil pipeline	Total
1950	602.3	46.2	23.4	20.1	4.9	696.9
1960	1,504.3	99.6	38.5	98.5	51.2	1,792.1
1961	1,566.6	106.0	40.4	105.7	60.0	1,878.7
1962	1,646.3	109.9	42.2	111.9	74.5	1,984.8
1963	1,749.4	114.5	45.4	119.7	90.9	2,119.9
1964	1,854.1	124.5	49.9	132.1	112.1	2,272.7
1965	1,948.0	133.9	52.1	142.7	146.6	2,423.3

Source: Holland Hunter, "The Soviet Transport Sector," in *New Directions in the Soviet Economy,* Studies Prepared for the Subcommittee on Foreign Economic Policy of the Joint Economic Committee, 89 Cong. 2 sess. (1966), p. 576.

TABLE A–10.   *Number of Trucks and Buses in Selected Countries, 1964*

Country	Trucks	Buses	Number of trucks per bus	Trucks per 1,000 inhabitants	Buses per 1,000 inhabitants
El Salvador	8,221	1,322	6.2	2.9	0.5
Mexico	352,681	27,573	12.8	9.5	0.7
Argentina	496,500	17,500	28.4	23.2	0.8
Brazil	655,874	72,534	9.0	8.7	1.0
Chile	82,548	9,149	9.0	10.3	1.1
India	219,591	73,176	3.0	0.5	0.2
Pakistan	21,137	9,753	2.2	0.2	0.1
Syria	12,043	1,753	6.9	2.3	0.3
Thailand	59,160	13,705	4.3	2.1	0.5
Ethiopia	5,032	961	5.2	0.2	0.05
Ghana	13,911	3,330	4.2	2.0	0.5
Sudan	16,540	1,393	11.9	1.3	0.1
Tanganyika	17,641	1,708	10.3	1.9	0.2
Japan	3,324,749	81,414	40.8	35.0	0.9
France	1,680,500	44,500	37.8	35.8	1.0
West Germany	712,600	34,100	20.9	13.0	0.6
Italy	547,878	30,406	18.0	10.9	0.6
Sweden	130,979	9,703	13.5	17.3	1.3
United Kingdom	1,571,800	84,700	18.6	29.4	1.6
United States	13,416,324	297,401	45.1	69.4	1.5

Source: U.S. Department of Commerce, Business and Defense Services Administration, *World Motor Vehicle Production and Registration, 1963–64* (January 1965).

TABLE A-11.   *Indian Rail Passenger Traffic, Suburban and Nonsuburban, 1950–65*
(In millions)

Year	Number of passengers			Passenger-kilometers		
	Suburban	Non-suburban	Total	Suburban	Non-suburban	Total
1950–51	. . .	. . .	1,284	. . .	. . .	66,517
1951–52	412	796	1,208	6,835	56,237	63,072
1955–56	499	776	1,275	8,165	54,235	62,400
1960–61	685	909	1,594	11,818	65,847	77,665
1961–62	764	928	1,692	13,268	68,617	81,885
1962–63	808	942	1,750	13,561	70,430	83,991
1963–64	882	990	1,872	14,460	74,128	88,588
1964–65	951	1,041	1,992	15,761	77,728	93,489
Percentage increase, 1950–65	131	31	55	131	38	41

Source: Government of India, Planning Commission, *Committee on Transport Policy and Coordination: Final Report* (1966), p. 12.

TABLE A-12.   *Domestic Air Passenger Services, Indian Airlines, 1955–65*

Year	Passenger-kilometers (in millions)	Number of passengers (in thousands)
1955–56	338	500
1960–61	614	787
1964–65	958	1,235
Percentage increase between 1955–56 and 1964–65	83	147

Source: Government of India, Planning Commission, *Committee on Transport Policy and Coordination: Final Report* (1966), p. 156.

TABLE A–13. *Selected Intercity Passenger Services in India, 1965*

Route	Railway Distance[a]	Railway Fare[b] First class	Railway Fare[b] Third class	Railway Travel time[c]	Road Distance[a]	Road Fare[b]	Road Travel time[c]	Air Fare[b]	Air Travel time[c]
Delhi-Bombay	1,388	99.3	32	23:20	1,398	. . .	. . .	232	1:55
Delhi-Madras	2,184	144.3	47	45:10	2,456	. . .	. . .	324	3:50
Delhi-Calcutta	1,441	100.6	33	24:15	1,426	. . .	. . .	255	2:05
Bombay-Calcutta	2,174	143.8	46	41:25	2,282	. . .	. . .	316	2:25
Bombay-Madras	1,278	90.8	30	27:30	1,354	. . .	. . .	278	1:40
Calcutta-Madras	1,694	113.1	37	33:45	1,653	. . .	. . .	258	2:10
Delhi-Amritsar	512	41.5	14	10:50	445	12.2	11:30	95	1:20
Delhi-Agra	196	17.0	6	3:30	203	5.4	5:30	41	0:40
Delhi-Jaipur	308	25.7	9	7:06	309	9.1	8:30	53	1:50

Source: Data supplied by the Planning Commission, Government of India.
a. In kilometers.
b. In rupees.
c. In hours and minutes.

TABLE A–14. *Cost of Transporting 20 Maunds of Groundnuts by Bullock Cart a Distance of 20 Miles*
(Time = 2 days)

Items in cost	Rupees
Bullock cart at 5 rupees per day	10.00
Expenses for 2 men for 2 days	
at 1.5 rupees per day	6.00
Expenses for feeding bullocks,	
at 2 rupees per day	4.00
Miscellaneous	2.00
Total	22.00
Cost for 20 miles per maund[a]	
(20 maunds transported)	1.10
Cost per maund per mile	0.055[b]

Source: A. K. Srivastava, "Market Study of Groundnuts (1963–64)" (Kanpur, 1965).
a. A maund = 82 pounds.
b. Or 20 cents (U.S.) per ton-mile, using long tons and the exchange rate of 7.5 rupees = 1 dollar.

TABLE A–15. *Cost of Transporting 150 Maunds of Groundnuts by Truck a Distance of 50 Miles*
(Time = 1 day)

Items in cost	Rupees
Charges per day at 1 rupee per maund	150.00
Loading and unloading at 1 rupee per day	3.75
Charges for 1 man for 2 days	3.00
Total	156.75
Cost for 50 miles per maund[a]	1.045
Cost per maund per mile	0.021[b]

Source: A. K. Srivastava, "Market Study of Groundnuts (1963–64)" (Kanpur, 1965).
a. A maund = 82 pounds.
b. Or about 8 cents (U.S.) per ton-mile, using long tons and the exchange rate of 7.5 rupees = 1 dollar.

TABLE A–16. *Access of Villages to Road System in Uttar Pradesh*
(In percent of total number of villages)

Region	On surfaced road	On unsurfaced road	On no road	All villages
Eastern	28.6	41.9	31.5	100
Central	28.7	34.7	36.6	100
Western	34.5	31.6	33.9	100
Hill	11.5	41.8	46.7	100
State as a whole	28.2	37.8	36.0	100

Source: Government of Uttar Pradesh, *Uttar Pradesh Transport Survey (Preliminary Report)* (Kanpur, February 1967).

TABLE A–17. *Estimated Cost of Proposed Educational TV Stations in the United States, 1980*

Elements in cost	Major stations		Other station types		
	Key	Regular	Standard	Basic	Repeater
Number of stations	20	40	75	75	170
Average population served per station (millions)	4	1	0.8	0.3	0.2
Population range of metropolitan areas served (millions)	1.2–15.0	Up to 1.8	0.3–1.0	0.1–0.3	. . .[a]
Number of studios	3	2	1	1	0
Capital required (million dollars)	6.2	3.3	1.7	1.3	0.55
Annual operating costs	3.0	1.2	0.49	0.16	0.038
Annual capital costs	0.1	0.3	0.16	0.13	0.047
Total costs per year	3.1	1.5	0.65	0.29	0.085

Source: *Public Television: A Program for Action,* The Report of the Carnegie Commission on Educational Television (Bantam Books, 1967), p. 142.

a. Does not serve a metropolitan area.

Index

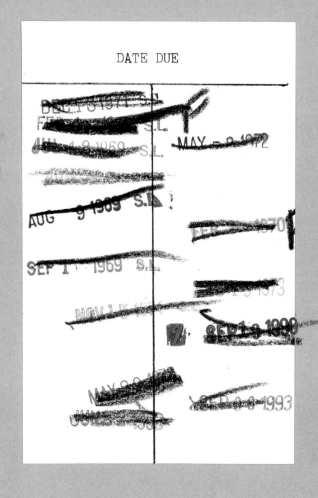

DATE DUE